SOLDIERS HOME, MEMPHIS, TENN.

ESTABLISHED BY THE WESTERN SANITARY COMMISSION, FEBRUARY 1st 1863.

THE

Western Sanitary Commission;

A SKETCH

OF ITS ORIGIN, HISTORY, LABORS FOR THE SICK AND WOUNDED OF THE WESTERN ARMIES, AND AID GIVEN TO FREEDMEN AND UNION REFUGEES, WITH INCIDENTS OF HOSPITAL LIFE.

ST. LOUIS:
PUBLISHED FOR THE MISSISSIPPI VALLEY SANITARY FAIR.
R. P. STUDLEY & CO.
1864.

CONTENTS.

CHAPTER I.

CHAPTER II.

CHAPTER III.

CHAPTER IX.

CHAPTER X.

CHAPTER XI.

THE

Western Sanitary Commission.

CHAPTER I.

ORIGIN OF SANITARY COMMISSIONS—HOW THE WESTERN COMMISSION CAME TO BE ORGANIZED—THE EARLY BATTLES IN MISSOURI—WANT OF PREPARATION FOR TAKING CARE OF THE WOUNDED—ORDER OF MAJ. GEN. FREMONT CONSTITUTING A SANITARY COMMISSION—ESTABLISHMENT OF MILITARY HOSPITALS IN ST. LOUIS—HOSPITAL CARS FITTED UP ON THE PACIFIC R. R.—VOLUNTARY CONTRIBUTIONS FROM NEW ENGLAND AND THE NORTH-WESTERN STATES—LOYAL SYMPATHIES AND PATRIOTISM OF THE WOMEN OF THE COUNTRY—INCIDENTS.

THE first organized attempt to mitigate the horrors of war, to prevent disease and save the lives of those engaged in military service, by sanitary measures and a more careful nursing of the sick and wounded, was made by a commission appointed by the British Government during the Crimean war, to inquire into the terrible mortality from disease that attended the British army at Sebastopol, and to apply the needed remedies. It was as a part of this great work that the heroic young Englishwoman, Florence Nightingale, with her army of nurses, went to the Crimea to care for the sick and wounded soldier, to minister in hospitals, and to alleviate suffering and pain, with a self-sacrifice and devotion that has made her name a household word, wherever the English language is spoken. In the armies of France the Sisters of Charity had rendered similar services, and even ministered to the wounded on the battle field; but their labors were a work of religious charity and not an organized sanitary movement.

The experience of armies having shown that not less than five soldiers die of disease to every one killed in battle, it became a problem, whether this immense loss could not be greatly diminished by sanitary means, and the military strength of a people be proportionally increased by a greater economy of life, and the superior health, vigor, and aggressive power of its armies. To this consideration was also added the Christian duty of a people to minister to the comfort and health of men engaged in so perilous a service, leaving their homes and families and kindred to encounter sickness, wounds, and death, for the sake of country and liberty.

The result of the enquiries of the British Commission, and of the researches of medical science has clearly established the fact that the "efficiency of an army must ever depend upon the state of health of the corps which compose it;" and that "the history of war can no longer be confined to bare details of the plans of battles and the manœuvres of armies," but that "we must refer to other elements, and principally to the sanitary condition of troops as the causes of our victories, or the reasons for our disasters." *

The idea of an organization of civilians to look after the health of the armies of the United States, on the breaking out of the present war, and to minister to the sick and wounded, when the great battles should be fought, which it was foreseen must be the inevitable results of the conflict, originated in the minds of humane and patriotic men, who had the welfare of the country, and its noble defenders, at heart, and took form in the summer and autumn of 1861, in the formation of the United States Sanitary Commission, with its centre of operations at Washington, and of the Western Sanitary Commission, with its field of service at St. Louis, and in the armies, the navy and the hospitals of the west.

The noble labors of the U. S. Commission and its subordinate

---

* The British Army and Miss Nightingale. By Charles Shrimpton, M. D., late Surgeon Major in the French Army, London: Bailliere Brothers, 1864. Quoted in North American Review, April, 1864.

branches having been already recorded in a valuable history,* and in various publications, it is proposed in the present publication to give a sketch of the Western Commission, its modes of operation, its agencies and labors in the western armies and hospitals, its incidental work for the Freedman and Union refugees, and its plans of usefulness for the future of the war.

The organization of the Western Sanitary Commission was the result of circumstances growing out of the war in Missouri; the necessity for it was both sudden and unexpected, and its earliest labors were entirely spontaneous and unpremeditated. The city of Saint Louis had become the Headquarters of the Military Department of the West. During the summer of 1861 the battles of Boonville, Dug Spring, Carthage, and Wilson's Creek, were fought in Missouri, the last on the 10th of August, twelve miles south of Springfield, near the Fayetteville road. This was one of the most desperately fought engagements of the war, and the number of killed and wounded was very great. The wounded, numbering 721, were brought all the way from Springfield to Rolla in ambulances and army wagons, and thence by cars to Saint Louis, and so little preparation had then been made for such an event that there were not additional hospital accommodations for so many in the whole city. The "New House of Refuge Hospital," situated two miles south of St. Louis, had only been opened on the 6th of the same month, by Medical Director De Camp, with Dr. Bailley in charge, two excellent and humane surgeons of the regular army, and was as yet unfinished and unprovided with the requisites of a good hospital. Its condition at the time is thus described in an article in the North American Review for April, 1864, entitled "Loyal Work in Missouri." "It had neither stoves, nor bedsteads, nor beds, nor bedding, nor food, nor nurses, nor any thing prepared. The first hundred arrived

---

*The United States Sanitary Commission, Boston; Little, Brown Company, 1863.

at night. They had been brought in wagons a hundred and twenty miles, over a rough road, by hurried marches, suffering for food and water, from Springfield to Rolla, and thence by rail to Saint Louis to the station on Fourteenth Street. There, having had nothing to eat for ten hours, they were put into furniture carts (much better than those instruments of torture called ambulances) and carried the remaining three miles. Bare walls, bare floors, and an empty kitchen received them ; but the kind-hearted surgeon, Bailley, did all he could to make kindness take the place of good fare. He obtained from the neighbors cooked food for their supper, and lost no time in getting together the various means of comfort. The poor fellows were so shattered and travel-worn that they were thankful enough to get eatable food, with the hard boards to sleep upon, and no word of complaint did we ever hear one of them utter. In the course of the week three or four hundred more were brought in, the condition of things meanwhile rapidly improving ; but so great was the difficulty of obtaining anything that was wanted, that many of the badly wounded men lay there in the same unchanged garments in which they had been brought from the battle-field three weeks before. Every day, however, made things better, and by the end of a month from the first arrivals Dr. Bailley began to say that 'it was not yet what he called a good hospital, but that the men were all comfortable.' "

Arrivals of sick and wounded continued and other accommodations had to be obtained without delay. All the available wards of the Saint Louis Hospital, kept by the Sisters of Charity, and of the City Hospital were immediately taken and filled, and still there was need of more hospitals. The sad and neglected condition of those who were brought from Springfield excited the benevolent and patriotic sympathies of all who loved their country and its brave defenders. The wounds of many had not been dressed since their first dressing after the battle ; others were still suffering from unextracted bullets and pieces of shell, and the hospitals were unprovided with the necessary hospital clothing to substitute for the soiled clothing of the men, which in many instances were saturated with the blood of their wounds.

It was at this juncture that the Western Sanitary Commission was suddenly called into existence. Miss D. L. Dix, the philanthropist, was then in Saint Louis, and in communication with the new Commander of the Department, Major General Fremont; Mrs. Fremont was also deeply interested in every thing relating to the welfare of the sick and wounded soldier; other persons of humane and patriotic motives and sentiments were personally known to General Fremont, and the suggestion of a Sanitary Commission at Saint Louis, to be subordinate to and act in aid of the Medical Department, coming from such sources, was favorably regarded and carried into immediate effect. An order was issued by him on the 5th of September, appointing the Western Sanitary Commission, in which its duties and sphere of action were thus defined:

"Its general object shall be to carry out, under the properly constituted military authorities, and in compliance with their orders, such sanitary regulations and reforms as the well-being of the soldiers demand.

"This Commission shall have authority—*under the directions of the Medical Director*—to select, fit up and furnish suitable buildings for Army and Brigade Hospitals, in such places and in such manner as circumstances require. It will attend to the selection and appointment of women nurses, under the authority and by the direction of Miss D. L. Dix, General Superintendent of the Nurses of Military Hospitals in the United States. It will co-operate with the surgeons of the several hospitals in providing male nurses, and in whatever manner practicable, and by their consent. It shall have authority to visit the different camps, to consult with the commanding officers, and the colonels and other officers of the several regiments, with regard to the sanitary and general condition of the troops, and aid them in providing proper means for the preservation of health and prevention of sickness, by supply of wholesome and well cooked food, by good systems of drainage, and other practicable methods. It will obtain from the community at large such additional means of increasing the comfort and promoting the moral and social welfare of the men, in camp and hospital, as may be needed, and cannot be furnished by Government Regulations. It will, from time to time, report directly to the Commander-in-Chief of the Department the condition of the camps and hospitals, with such suggestions as can properly be made by a Sanitary Board.

"This Commission is not intended in any way to interfere with the Medical Staff, or other officers of the army, but to co-operate with them, and aid them in the discharge of their present arduous and extraordinary duties. It will be treated by all officers of the army, both regular and volunteer, in this Department, with the respect due to the humane and patriotic motives of the members, and to the authority of the Commander-in-Chief.

"This Sanitary Commission will, for the present, consist of James E. Yeatman, Esq.; C. S. Greeley, Esq.; J. B. Johnson, M. D.; George Partridge, Esq., and the Rev. Wm. G. Eliot, D. D."

As soon as this order was issued the gentlemen named in it, acting as a Sanitary Commission, commenced their labors in connection with the Medical Department. Their first important work was the fitting up of a new hospital sufficiently large to accommodate at least five hundred patients. Negotiations were opened for renting the large five story marble-fronted building, corner of Fifth and Chesnut streets, which was secured at a reasonable rent. Necessary alterations were made, arrangements for bathing introduced, special diet-kitchens were fitted up, and the whole building furnished with beds and bedding. On the 10th of September it was opened for the reception of patients, under the charge of Surgeon John T.

Hodgen, U. S. V., with a competent corps of Assistant Surgeons, apothecary, steward, ward masters, nurses, &c., under the title of the "City General Hospital."

It was rapidly filled with patients and continued as a military hospital until the autumn of 1863, under the charge of Dr. Hodgen, whose able and faithful services and great surgical skill were fully recognized and appreciated by the Medical Department and by the Western Sanitary Commission, with whom his relations have always been most intimate, and whose members have ever found in him a willing co-worker and friend.

Being located in a central part of the city, convenient to the rail road depots and the river, it was the place of reception of nearly all the severely wounded and the hopelessly sick on their arrival, for which reasons its per centage of deaths was large, being 14½ for a period of nearly two years ; but it was one of the best conducted and well managed hospitals in the west.

It was in this building the Western Sanitary Commission commenced its useful and arduous labors, havlng its office in a small room at the left of the entrance, in the second story, and a store room for sanitary goods in the basement, its members meeting every day for consultation and action; its President, Jas. E. Yeatman, giving his whole time to the work, and having only one man to act as store keeper, porter and clerk, at the small salary of thirty dollars a month ; and yet the work went on, each member of the Commission lending a helping hand, boxes of sanitary stores arriving from New England, and from the various towns and cities of the West, prepared and forwarded by the willing hands of the wives and mothers and daughters of the land, and being distributed as needed to the hospitals and camps, and regiments in and around St. Louis, and at more distant posts in the interior of the State.

From September 12th to September 21st, occurred the seige, the battle, and surrender of Lexington, Mo., which threw some three hundred more wounded men upon the hospitals of St. Louis. During the two months in which these events happened, besides the hospitals already named, five more were added, the Good Samaritan, the Fourth Street or Eliot Hospital, the Pacific, the Post and the Convalescent Hospitals at Benton Barracks.

During the month of October, Maj. Gen. Fremont took the field in person, with an army of twenty thousand troops, and went in pursuit of the rebel Gen. Price, who had retreated from Lexington. This pursuit was continued to Springfield, Mo., under forced marches, and on Gen. Fremont's removal from the command, November 5th, the army was ordered back again by the new commander, Maj. Gen. Hunter. By this long and toilsome march and counter march, many of the troops were broken down, and were transferred to the hospitals.

One of the last acts that Gen. Fremont performed, on leaving St Louis on this expedition, was an order, alike creditable to his judgment and his humanity, directed to the Western Sanitary Commission, to fit up two hospital cars on the Pacific Railroad, with berths, nurses, cooking arrangements, etc., for the transportation of the sick and wounded, which was done. These were probably the first hospital cars prepared and furnished as such in the United States, and for several months they proved exceedingly useful.

Through all these exciting months the members of the Western Sanitary Commission continued their voluntary labors without abatement, and the fitting up of all these hospitals was left mainly to them by the then acting Medical Director. As sanitary stores were needed, appeals were made through the newspapers and generously responded to by the people of St. Louis. Gradually the work of the Commission became more widely known; some of its members having a large acquaintance in New England, an interest was excited there, and contributions of hospital clothing, bandages, lint, dried and canned fruits, jellies and other delicacies for the sick, began to arrive from that source, and from Wisconsin, Iowa, Illinois, Michigan, and other Western States. From the principal cities and towns of Massachusetts, New Hampshire, and Rhode Island; from Boston, Providence and Portsmouth; from Salem, New Bedford, Worcester, Springfield, Cambridge, Cambridgeport, Roxbury, Newton, and many other towns, boxes came filled with new blankets, sheets, comforters, pillows, towels, socks, mittens, bandages, lint, and many little articles of convenience for the soldier's private use, such as needle books, pin cushions, handkerchiefs, games for amusement, little boxes of salve for sores and wounds, all showing the thoughtful sympathy and affection of the noble women of the country for those who had taken up arms to vindicate the majesty or the Government against a most unholy rebellion—a cause in which their own fathers, husbands, brothers, and sons had enlisted that they might preserve the institutions of liberty to themselves and coming generations.

It was an interesting spectacle to see these boxes opened in the store rooms of the Commission, and on examination to find in the socks and mittens (of which there were many thousand pairs, in anticipation of the needs of the winter,) tracts and manuscript letters, full of words of advice, encouragement and sympathy. Sometimes there would be found in the toe of a sock a letter addressed, "To the soldier who shall wear these socks: Be of good cheer! may these socks keep your feet warm, while you stand on your post, or march on to battle and victory!" "May the rebellion soon be subdued, and you have the satisfaction of having aided in the glorious work." Sometimes quite lengthy epistles would be folded up in these presents, with the names and address of the writers given, and we have known some very pleasant correspondence to follow from these friendly missives to the soldiers. In one instance a pocket bible was contained among the sanitary stores, having the name and address of the giver, and was given to an intelligent and faithful soldier at Rolla, who wrote the lady an acknowledgment of the gift, and a very interesting and profitable correspondence resulted.

Sometimes these presents would contain a slip of paper, on which would be written, "Knit by a little girl, eight years of age," and sometimes another would be written, "Knit by E—— F——, aged seventy-six years," showing that from childhood to age the women of the country, were heart and hand with their country's defenders, in the war for the preservation of the Union.

From the Northwestern States contributions also came in freely, especially from Wisconsin, where the Rev. H. A. Reid, and his wife, devoted themselves, with a truly Christian zeal, to the work of soliciting supplies. Illinois and Iowa, and Michigan also did their part nobly, and a few gifts were sent from Ohio, though the contributions from that State went mostly to the U. S. Sanitary Commission. The supplies sent from these Western States were largely of canned and dried fruits, jellies, butter, etc., for the use of the sick. In this connection the City of Madison, and all the smaller towns in Wisconsin, the cities of Chicago, Quincy, Alton, Peoria, and the smaller towns in Illinois; the cities of Detroit, Ypsilanti, Marshall, Battle Creek, and other places in Michigan, the cities of Davenport, Dubuque, Keokuk, and the towns of Iowa will be long and gratefully remembered.

CHAPTER II.

CHANGE OF DEPARTMENT COMMANDERS IN THE WEST—GENERAL HALLECK—LARGE INCREASE OF TROOPS—HOSPITALS FILLED—NEW HOSPITALS OPENED—PREVALENCE OF MEASLES, PNEUMONIA, TYPHOID FEVER AND DIARRHEA DURING THE FALL AND WINTER OF 1861-2—LARGE ARRIVALS AND DISTRIBUTIONS OF SANITARY STORES—INSPECTION OF HOSPITALS—SECRETARYSHIP OF THE COMMISSION—MEDICAL DIRECTOR, J. J. B. WRIGHT—DEFICIENCY OF THE MEDICAL SUPPLY TABLE—THE LABORS OF THE LOYAL AND PATRIOTIC WOMEN OF ST. LOUIS IN THE HOSPITALS—THE EMPLOYMENT OF FEMALE NURSES—THEIR HEROISM AND SELF-SACRIFICE.

On the removal of Maj. Gen. Fremont, his successor continued in command but sixteen days, when he was superseded by the appointment of Maj. Gen. Halleck on the 21st of November. The business of recruiting, which had suffered on account of these changes, was now revived and carried forward successfully, until there were encamped at Benton Barracks, during the months of December and January, 1861–'62, over twenty thousand troops, infantry, cavalry, and artillery, from nearly all the Western States. The extensive grounds and barracks prepared by General Fremont were entirely occupied, and the work of military instruction went forward with zeal and energy.

The presence of so many troops in one great encampment, the crowded condition of the barracks, the inexperience of the soldiers in their first encounter with exposure and hardship, the inclemency of the winter months, and the inability of the department to do all that was required, occasioned a large amount of sickness among the different regiments. The most prevalent diseases were measles, pneumonia, typhoid fever, and diarrhea. In one instance, it happened that three hundred, in a single regiment of cavalry, were sick, mostly taken down with measles. In another, the surgeon reported one thousand out of thirteen hundred men, suffering from coughs and colds. The barracks being rough buildings, with many open cracks, and floors without any space beneath, were far from comfortable, and the regimental hospitals were not well warmed, nor kept at an even temperature, nor properly ventilated. The consequence was that many of the measle patients were afterwards attacked with pneumonia, and died. The small-pox also broke out, and the hospital established on Duncan's Island, (opposite the arsenal, in the Mississippi river,) for this class of patients, was filled and required additional accommodations.

During the months of December and January, the number of sick and wounded in all the hospitals of Saint Louis and vicinity had reached over 2,000, and the labors of the Sanitary Commission were greatly increased. Meetings were held every few days; frequent inspections were made of all the hospitals and camps; reports were prepared and submitted to the commanding general; improvements were introduced; and supplies were forwarded wherever needed.

Besides the hospitals and camps in and around Saint Louis, there were large bodies of troops at Rolla, the terminus of the south-west branch of the Pacific railroad, a point of great strategic importance, and at Tipton and Sedalia, two other important points, and at Ironton, the southern terminus of the Iron Mountain railroad, and at Jefferson City, the capital of the State, where they were encamped for the winter. At these places there was a large amount of sickness and great mortality. The tents and huts in which the soldiers had gone into win ter quarters, were poorly ventilated; the hospitals were generally log buildings, very much crowded, badly ventilated, and yet allowing the entrance of draughts of cold air, having also bad floors, through which the dampness ascended from the ground. The soldiers were not yet inured to hardship, and were inexperienced in taking proper care of themselves, and in attending to sanitary and police regulations, and the consequence was a melancholy state of disease and death at those military posts. The writer of this sketch has a sad remembrance of the new-made graves at Rolla, which he found there in the spring of 1862, where so many of the Iowa, and Illinois and Missouri troops spent the fall and early part of winter before they went on their victorious march, under General Curtis, through Springfield to Pea Ridge, recovering the ground relinquished by Gen. Hunter, after the removal of Fremont, and driving the rebels from Missouri beyond the Boston Mountains.

But before this march was undertaken, and while the troops lay in their winter encampments, the demands for sanitary stores were incessant, and the supply was always equal to the emergency. From regimental surgeons there was a constant application for additional medicines beyond the allowance afforded by the Medical Department. The old medical supply table was found utterly inadequate to the emergency. Expectorants and other important remedies were in constant demand, and large additions were furnished by the Sanitary Commission. The request was equally urgent for hospital clothing and delicate food for the sick. Large issues were made of blankets, sheets, pillows, pillow slips, comforters, slippers, socks, wrappers, shirts, drawers, bandages, lint, and supplies of farina, jellies, canned and dried fruits, stimulants, &c. Surgeons came into the Sanitary Rooms personally to present their requests, and voluntary agents from Rolla, Jefferson City, Tipton, Sedalia, and Ironton al so came, and represented the condition of the hospitals at those posts, to all of which liberal responses were made, goods forwarded, visits made in person by the President and members of the Commission, and members of the Ladies' Union Aid Society, and every thing done that was possible to alleviate suffering and diminish disease.

In these labors the Western Commission received the hearty and cordial support of Major General Halleck, the new commander of the Western Department, and was often favored with the presence at its meetings of his Chief of Staff, Brigadier General George W. Cullum, U. S. A., whose experience and excellent suggestions were of great value.

Up to this period, January, 1862, the Commission had received over five hundred and twenty-five boxes of goods, and distributed over fifteen thousand articles, consisting of hospital clothing, and delicate preparations of food for the sick, besides aiding to furnish many of the general hospitals and supplying the deficiencies of medicine to the regiments.

The work of the Commission during the months of December and January had consisted largely in the visitation and inspection of the camps and hospitals in and around Saint Louis, in efforts for their improvement, in the reception and distribution of sanitary stores, in the employment of female nurses, and in correspondence with the military authorities and the friends of the Union cause in different parts of the country.

In the enlargement of its work it became necessary to procure additional store room for goods, and to employ a Secretary. For a period of three months this position was filled by Rev. J. G. Forman, of Alton, Ill., who resigned it to enter upon his duties as Chaplain of the 3d Missouri volunteers, and Mr. L. B. Ripley succeeded him for several months, when he also resigned and became the Quartermaster of the 33d Missouri volunteers. In May, 1863, Rev. Mr. Forman again became permanently Secretary of the Commission.

In February, 1862, the small room in the Fifth Street Hospital was vacated for the larger rooms, No. 10, North Fifth Street, still occupied by the Commission.

In the month of December the excellent Medical Director, Surgeon De Camp, with whom the Commission had labored in establishing and fitting up the new military hospitals, was superseded by Dr. J. J. B. Wright, U. S. A., and it was some time before the relations of the Commission became entirely harmonious with this officer. Like many of the old army surgeons he was sensitive of any imaginary interference with the Medical Department, considered it fully competent to manage every thing relating to the health of the army, and had an evident dislike of sanitary commissions, and a disposition to decline all aid from this source. He was in the habit of remarking that the old army had never received any such assistance, and that he saw no reason why the volunteers should have this partiality shown to them. But the Sanitary Commission showed no partialities, and all soldiers of the United States, whether regulars or volunteers, were treated by it precisely alike. The prejudice existing in the minds of the surgeons of the regular army towards the Sanitary Commissions and the surgeons of the volunteer forces has been frequently manifested, and is to be greatly deplored, preventing harmony of action and resulting in much injury to the service.

In the present instance there was great complaint from the surgeons of the volunteer regiments of the deficiency of the medical supply table, and constant applications were made to the Commission for additional medicines. The regimental surgeons stated that they could not get their requisitions answered at the medical purveyor's office; that the articles they most needed were stricken off, the quantities reduced in others, and that their patients could not be properly treated and were dying for want of proper medicines. The difficulty was represented to Maj. Gen. Halleck by the Commission, and he issued an order on the Medical Department to increase its allowances, which order the Medical Director refused to comply with. The matter was referred by Gen. Halleck to Washington, and the result was that in the end the medical supply table for regiments in the field was considerably enlarged. The relations of the Commission afterwards became more harmonious with Medical Director Wright, as he found its services to be really useful and necessary; but, although invited, he never attended its meetings, and always maintained a distant and merely official intercourse with its members.

While the Commission was thus engaged the loyal and patriotic women of the city were not less active, in works of love for the sick and wounded, and in expressions of encouragement and sympathy for the soldiers in the field. In them the Commission found most energetic and faithful co-workers. At the rooms of the Ladies' Union Aid and of the Fremont Relief Societies, they met daily and cut out hospital garments, employed sewing machines in the making of them, gave occupation and assistance to soldiers' wives and families, received and distributed sanitary stores, visited the sick, carrying with them delicately prepared food and cordials, good religious books, and other reading matter to cheer and comfort them, conversed at their bedsides, gave them consolation and sympathy, and in many instances gave hope in Christ and confidence in God and heaven to the departing spirit. The labors thus cheerfully performed will not only find an honorable record on earth, but are already registered in heaven.

It would be a grateful task to the writer to name many of those whom he often met in these visitations of mercy in the hospitals, but the fear of wounding by giving publicity to deeds that were not done to secure the world's applauses, and making omissions that would seem like an unjust discrimination, induces him to refrain from the attempt. Some of them were the wives of our best and most loyal citizens, persons of wealth, culture and refinement, who used to sit for hours by the bed-side of the sick and wounded, fanning the fevered brow, reading from some good book, and speaking so hopefully, that their gentle influence was always visible in its effects upon the countenances of those who were the objects of their tender solicitude and care. In one instance, a youth, hardly yet more than a boy, who had been often visited, as his spirit was sinking away from earth, asked one of these goodly women to kiss him for his mother; and the farewell kiss was given, and the spirit of the boy departed, leaving the smile of peace on his fair young face, which his own dear mother could never kiss again.

Among those who thus passed from room to room through the hospitals, giving to one a testament, to another a soldier's prayer-book, to a third a volume of pleasant reading, accompanied always by an expression of friendly interest and sympathy, two sisters from Philadelphia are warmly remembered, who came all the way to Saint Louis, and spent the winter in these holy ministries of love, whose names, like the true sisters of humanity of our own city, I leave unmentioned here, feeling assured that they are all recorded in the Lamb's Book of Life, and written on the tablet of many a soldier's heart.

The following lines, written by a private soldier, addressed to one who had thus ministered to him in sickness, are the fit expression of what was often conveyed in the pleased and grateful countenance of many a sick and dying soldier to the saintly souls of those who came to bless and comfort them in their hours of pain and languishing:

"From old Saint Paul 'till now,
Of honorable women, not a few
Have left their golden ease in love to do
The saintly work which Christ-like hearts pursue.

"And such an one art thou! God's fair apostle,
Bearing His love in war's horrific train:
Thy blessed feet follow its ghastly pain —
And misery, and death, without disdain.

"To one borne from the sullen battle's roar,
Dearer the greeting of thy gentle eyes,
When he, aweary, torn and bleeding lies,
Than all the glory that the victors prize!

"When peace shall come, and homes shall smile again,
A thousand soldier-hearts in northern climes,
Shall tell their little children in their rhymes,
Of the sweet saints who blessed the old war times."

The employment of female nurses, and their assignment to duty in the hospitals, was another important service rendered by the President of the commission—a delicate trust—and one attended with many difficulties. The example of Florence Nightingale and her corps of female nurses in the Crimea, and the patriotic sympathies of the women of America with their brothers in arms, led large numbers of them to offer themselves for this service. The natural superiority of women, as nurses, was felt by all, and the government, therefore, determined to make room for a certain proportion of female nurses in the hospitals. Miss D. L. Dix, a lady widely and favorably known by her humanitary labors for prisoners and the insane, was appointed "Superintendent of Women Nurses," to determine upon their qualifications, and grant certificates; and only those who had received such certificates, either from her or her agents, were to be employed by the surgeons in charge of general hospitals. The President of the Western Sanitary Commission was made the agent of Miss Dix for the Western Department, and on him the duty devolved of receiving all applications for this branch of the service, determining the qualifications of the applicants, granting the certificates of appointment, and assigning them to duty in the hospitals, on the request of the surgeons in charge for the number required.

The qualifications of women nurses were, that the applicants should be of suitable age, (from 25 to 50 years,) that they should be persons in good health, with sound constitutions, capable of bearing fatigue; that they should be free from levity and frivolity, of an earnest but cheerful spirit; that they should dress in plain colors, and in a manner convenient for their work; that they should be persons of good education; and, that they should be recommended by at least two responsible persons, (their clergyman and physician being preferred,) as to their fitness for this service.

At a later period Surgeon General Wm. A. Hammond issued an order regulating the number of women nurses to be employed in the general hospitals to one for every twenty beds, afterwards modified to one for every thirty beds, and requiring that no nurses should be employed without the certificate of Miss Dix, or her agents, except on emergencies.

Under these regulations a large number of women nurses were employed in the hospitals of the Western Department, and were allowed a compensation of $12 per month and transportation from their place of residence, and to it again on their being relieved from duty, with quarters and a ration (or board) in the hospitals. The full number allowed was seldom called for by the surgeons, and in some of the more distant hospitals the regulations were not always complied with, the surgeons in charge often employing persons selected by themselves, and not always such as would have been approved. This practice has recently been prevented by an order from the War Department, prohibiting the payment of all who have not received the proper certificates of approval from Miss Dix, or from those acting with her authority.

The nurses commissioned by the President of the Western Sanitary Commission have generally been such as to do honor to the service, and by their devotion to the sick and wounded soldier, their attention to his diet, their oversight of his welfare, their watchings by his bedside, their kindly presence and cheering influence, they have often turned the balance when poised between life and death, and saved many a soldier and hero to his country and his friends.

The number employed in the hospitals of the Western Department up to the present date, (May, 1864,) holding their certificates from the President of the Western Commission, is two hundred and seventy-three.* A few instances of unworthiness have occurred, and

* In giving this account of women nurses it is proper to state that an order was issued from the Medical Department in October, 1863, directing that certificates should be granted to those nurses who had been for some time in the service, on the recommendation of the surgeons in charge. Under this order about one hundred certificates were sent by mail in answer to such recommendations. It has been since ascertained that some of those for whom certificates were thus obtained were cooks and laundresses, the surgeons in these cases taking the responsibility as to the character of those whom they recommended.

some have failed to meet the requirements of the situation, but generally they have been persons of intelligence, good education, and a credit to humanity, the noblest types "of good, heroic womanhood." Many of them have left homes of comfort and refinement, and the pleasant associations of honored friends and kindred, to engage in this work of self-sacrifice ; some have been closely related to the best and noblest families in the nation, and left all to minister in hospitals for the sake of those who have fought and bled in the sacred cause of human liberty. Others again, have laid down their lives in this holy service, dying of disease incurred in the infected air of the hospital, and passing onward with our departed heroes and martyrs to that higher life where the sounds of war and conflict are hushed in eternal peace.

CHAPTER III.

The Battle of Fort Donelson—Activity of the Western Sanitary Commission—Steamers employed to bring the wounded to the Saint Louis Hospitals—A Delegation from the Commission and the Ladies' Union Aid Society return with a load of the Wounded—Attentions to the Sick—The first suggestion of Hospital Steamers—The Western Sanitary Commission Immediately acted on the suggestion—The "City of Louisiana" fitted up for this service—First trip to Island No. 10—Value and Usefulness of Hospital Steamers proved by Subsequent Experience—Assistant Surgeon-General R. C. Wood—Great Demand for Surgeons and Nurses—James M. Barnard, Esq., of Boston—Battle of Pea Ridge—Destitute condition of the Sick and Wounded—The Hospitals at Cassville—A. W. Plattenburg sent by the Commission with Sanitary Stores—Interesting Account of his Journey and of the Good Accomplished by it—The Agency Continued—His Future Labors—Testimonials of his Usefulness—Heroism of Mrs. Phelps at Pea Ridge.

On the 13th, 14th, and 15th of February, 1862, was fought the battle of Fort Donelson, on the Cumberland River in West Tennessee, in which the United States forces under General U. S. Grant, were victorious, compelling the surrender of the Fort, and taking 10,000 prisoners of war under the rebel Brig. Gen. S. B. Buckner. In this battle there were 231 killed and 1,007 wounded of the Confederate forces, and the loss on our own side was much greater, as the rebels fought within their entrenchments and our troops in the open field, where for three nights they lay upon the bare ground in a driving storm of snow and sleet, and renewed the battle from day to day, till victory crowned their arms.

On the news of this battle reaching St. Louis the Western Sanitary Commission made every preparation to assist the Medical Department in the care of the sick and wounded. A member of the Commission, accompanied by a delegation of physicians, nurses, and members of the Ladies' Union Aid Society, and by Surgeon J. H. Grove, U. S. V., proceeded immediately to Cairo by rail, and thence by steamer to Paducah, Ky., at the mouth of the Cumberland river, with sanitary stores, to which place the wounded had been brought, where they were most courteously received by Medical Director Simmons, who placed the steamer "*Ben Franklin*" at their service, and ordered a load of the wounded to be put in their charge to bring to St. Louis.

While the boat was being made ready, the ladies of the delegation went on board the various steamers at the landing and gave their kind attentions to the wounded, assisting to wash them, and to promote their comfort in every possible way.

The following account of the return trip is from the report made to the Commission at the time: "Furnished with the order of the Medical Director we visited the various hospitals in Paducah, and selected as many of the wounded as we could safely and comfortably transport to St. Louis. It required twenty-four hours to get 155 patients on board.

"As soon as we got under way, the ladies set to work to wash and cleanse, and comb the hair of the sick and wounded. Warm water, soap, sponge, and flesh brushes were brought in requisition. Not only the face and neck, but the hands and feet, and other parts of the body had to undergo this purifying process. After this, the surgeons, Drs. Grove, Alleyne, and myself, proceeded to dress the wounds and other severe injuries of our patients, in which again we were materially aided by the ladies and gentlemen of our delegation. This process required from three to four hours daily.

"The following was the daily routine: Early in the morning the ladies attended to the ablutions and cleansing of the patients. Breakfast was then served them, after which, a careful surgical and medical examination was gone through. Then came dinner, when they were waited on by all on board who could be spared from duty. After dinner, they were read to, and entertained by conversation. At supper again they had the attentions of all on board. After which we had singing of sacred or national hymns, reading the Scriptures, and prayer."

On arriving at St. Louis the wounded were at once taken in charge by medical officers, acting under the Medical Director, and transferred to the various hospitals.

From this time, general hospitals were established at Paducah and Mound City, and the Western Commission directed a portion of its supplies to those points, and many sanitary stores were also sent directly from the towns and cities of Illinois, accompanied by friends and relatives, and other humane persons, who went to tender their services as nurses, or in any capacity in which they could be useful.

It was during the trip of the St. Louis Sanitary delegation to Paducah, that the idea of hospital steamers was suggested by Dr. Simmons, the Medical Director, and embodied in the report to the Western Commission. He thought it would be wise to procure several good sized steamers and to fit them up as floating hospitals, properly organized with a chief surgeon, assistant surgeons, stewards, nurses, medical and sanitary stores, to accompany the progress of our arms along the western rivers, and to be always ready to receive the sick and wounded, on the occurrence of great battles, and convey them to the general hospitals, already provided farther north. The trip of the "*Ben. Franklin*" was itself a recommendation of the plan, and it was speedily acted upon by the Commission.

At the same meeting at which the above report and suggestions were made, Rev. Wm. G. Eliot, D.D., was requested to address a letter to Maj. Gen. Halleck, setting forth the proposed plan for one or more Floating Hospitals, pledging that the Commission, if the suggestion met with his approbation, would take the whole care and labor of carrying it into execution.

The plan was highly approved by the General commanding, and an order was issued to the chief quartermaster to purchase a steamer suited to the purpose, who, in connection with the Commission, finally selected and chartered the "*City of Louisiana*." On the 20th of March she had been thoroughly furnished as a hospital boat, the Government supplying her with beds and commissary stores, and the Western Sanitary Commission completing her outfit at an expense of $3000. In addition to this the Commission also provided the assistant surgeons, the apothecary, the male and female nurses, and furnished a full supply of sanitary stores. Her first trip was made to Island No. 10, to await the conflict there, but the place was taken at last by a flank movement of Gen. Pope on New Madrid, without loss of life, and there was no occasion for her service at that time. But it was not long till ample opportunity of usefulness occurred at Pittsburg Landing. On this first trip the President of the Western Sanitary Commission went also, sharing in the general expectation of a terrible battle at Island No. 10.

After the battle of Pittsburg Landing this boat conveyed 3,389 patients to northern hospitals, and was in the spring of 1863, purchased by the Government, remodeled for a permanent floating hospital, with accommodations for five hundred beds, and named the "*R. C. Wood,*" in honor of the Assistant Surgeon General of the United States Army, who was the first of the leading surgeons of the regular army to give his sanction and approval to the plan of a Sanitary Commission, and has always given his influence, encouragement, and aid to its beneficent labors, counselled with its members, and carried into effect, in his department, every valuable suggestion it has made.

The "*R. C. Wood*" is a vessel of great speed, and of large dimensions. Her state rooms have been removed, and the whole upper deck made into one large ward, with abundant light admitted, and having excellent means of ventilation, with ample provision of bath rooms, hot and cold water, cooking apartments, nurses' rooms, medical dispensary, laundry, and many other conveniences. With all the requisites of a good hospital on shore, it has the advantage of the fresh breezes and currents of air that are common to the river; and in the heat of summer, by moving on the stream, a delightful ventilation and refreshing breeze are obtained, passing through the sick ward, and cooling the fevered brows and pulses of the patients on board. During the summer of 1863 this boat made constant trips from the army at Vicksburg, bringing the wounded and sick to the St. Louis hospitals. During her first period of service she was in charge of Dr. Wagener, and is now in charge of Surgeon Thomas F. Azpell, U. S. V. The great utility and valuable service of floating hospitals was soon established and led to the fitting out of several others by the Government.

During the month of February, 1862, the Western Commission distributed 13,250 articles of hospital clothing, food for the sick, bottles of cordials and stimulants, packages of bandages and lint, crutches, back-rests for supporting the head and shoulders, splints, towels, bandages, socks, slippers, books, and packages of reading matter; and the labors of its members were constant and unceasing, frequently occupying the night as well as the day.

The demand for nurses was at this time very great. From the Mound City Hospital, near Cairo, Ill., in charge of Surgeon E. C. Franklin, U. S. V., there was a request at one time for forty nurses, of which only fourteen could be immediately sent. Several surgeons were proprocured from Boston, Mass., to come out and enter the hospital service, in which the commission had the valuable aid and recommendations of James M. Barnard, Esq., of that city, who has, in a thousand ways, assisted in its work, aided its contributions and given it his best influence and counsel.

On the 7th and 8th of March, 1862, another great battle was fought at Pea Ridge, Ark., in which our forces under Maj. Gen. S. R. Curtis, were victorious over a force of the enemy, three times our number, commanded by Generals Van Dorn, Price, McCulloch and McIntosh. Our killed and wounded numbered one thousand; the loss of the enemy was still greater. The great distance of this battle-field from St. Louis, being two hundred and fifty miles beyond Rolla, the terminus of the South-West Branch of the Pacific railroad, and the roads being of the very worst description, through a country only half-civilized, mountainous, without bridges, and without hotel accommodations, stripped by the passage of armies of forage for teams and of food for men, subject to raids and murders by guerrilla bands, it was utterly impossible to bring the wounded of Gen. Curtis' army to the hospitals of St. Louis. And what was still worse, the march through the south-west had been undertaken in the winter, over bad roads, with deficient transportation, and the medical department was most miserably provided with the means of taking care of so many wounded. The surgeons were without hospital clothing, without stimulants, so necessary in surgical operations, without bedding for the wounded, and their supply of medicines was exceedingly limited.

The desperate character of the battle had suddenly thrown upon their hands nearly a thousand badly wounded men, in a country thinly settled by a people living mostly in log houses, and having few of the necessaries of life. The court house at Cassville, and all the principal dwellings—there was not a church in the place—were filled, and many wounded were also housed in the same way at Keitsville, so that on approaching these villages every other dwelling seemed to be a hospital, having a red flag floating over it.

In a few instances, wounded officers were conveyed in ambulances all the way to Rolla, and taken home to their friends; and those of our brave troops who were less severely wounded were transported to Springfield, Mo., where the churches and public buildings were converted into hospitals for their use. Passing onward from Rolla to the Army of the South-west, soon after the battle, with the Lyon regiment, to reinforce Gen. Curtis, it was a painful scene to witness wounded men lying in the bottom of open wagons on beds of straw, jolted over the rough ground, on their way to friends living along the route; for among the regiments that fought most bravely and suffered most severely, was Phelps' Missouri six months volunteers, composed of the sons of loyal families, who had lived and suffered in

South-west Missouri from the persecutions of the rebels, many of them having been driven to Rolla as a place of refuge and enlisted there, and such of them as now were wounded were being conveyed to their own homes, or to Springfield, where better hospital accommodations existed. In this city, as we marched through, we found the hospital buildings filled with the wounded from Pea Ridge; and at Cassville, when we reached there, it was a touching sight to behold, as we did, in one room, a row of young men, in the freshness of youth, lying on beds, each having lost a leg, while in other buildings were those who had received all manner of hurts, wounds from pieces of shell, bullet wounds, arms torn and afterwards amputated, and legs taken off, and all bound up, awaiting the dreadful issue of life or death.

But it was with peculiar satisfaction we found that the stores of the Western Sanitary Commission had been received there some days before our arrival, and that the wounded men were lying in clean beds, and clothed with shirts and drawers, instead of the blood-stained garments in which they came from the battle-field. The large supplies, forwarded by the commission, had reached the medical director, Dr. Otterson, and had been put to immediate use; his supply of stimulants had been largely increased, and his sick and wounded were in a comfortable condition.

On the news of this battle reaching St. Louis, the members of the Sanitary Commission worked day and night, packing up sanitary stores, and sent forward Mr. A. W. Plattenburg in charge of hospital supplies, on the 11th of March, who was followed immediately after by another supply of as many more. In this undertaking, Maj. Gen. Halleck furnished every facility in his power, giving to Mr. Plattenburg an order, over his own signature, addressed "to all quartermasters and other officers between St. Louis and Sugar Creek, Ark.," directing them "to furnish every reasonable facility in their power, to forward, *with all possible dispatch*, consistent with safety, the bearer, Mr. A. W. Plattenburg, and the hospital stores under his care, destined for the wounded in the late battle at Sugar Springs"—afterwards named Pea Ridge.

In his report of his journey and arrival at Cassville with his stores Mr. Plattenburg says:

"I arrived at Rolla, Mo., at four o'clock, P. M., of the same day and was furnished with a horse and transportation for sanitary stores. The first day we proceeded fifteen miles over a road that was as bad as it could be. The day following I rode forty miles and stopped at night with a Union man, who had been robbed of almost everything movable. He had two sons in Phelps' Missouri regiment, one of whom had just died in the Springfield hospital. On Sunday morning I reached Springfield at 10 A. M. The Quartermaster was ordered to furnish transportation by the first train. The wounded from the recent battle were coming in, as well as some rebel prisoners. I visited the post hospital, accompanied by Dr. Ebert. There were one hundred sick and wounded, mostly from Pea Ridge. I examined the hospital very carefully; found a part of the men on the floor, destitute of all comforts. They had neither bed sacks, blankets nor sheets, not even tin cups or a teapot. They were, however, very cheerful. Dr. Ebert, a very kind and attentive surgeon, requested me to procure a wardmaster and matron. I made a requisition upon your Commission for them, as also for a large number of supplies for the hospital, enough to make all the patients as comfortable as possible.

"The train with your stores reached Springfield on Wednesday following, and on Friday were sent forward. Transportation was so insufficient that this delay was unavoidable. The next day, 25th, I arrived at Cassville. Here I found two large tents, six buildings, (among them the court house,) and the tavern, used as hospitals. The patients were lying on the floors, with a little straw under them, and with knapsacks or blankets under their heads for pillows. They had no comforts of any kind, no change of clothes, but were lying in the clothes they fought in, stiff and dirty with blood and soil. There were four hundred federal wounded here. There was a great deficiency of nurses, detailed men not answering the purpose well. Their sheets had been torn up for bandages, and until Dr. Otterson reached there with his supplies they were poorly furnished with medicines. Stimulants were very much needed to sustain the sinking men, but none were to be had. There were no brooms to sweep with and no mops to wash the rooms. Your stores were here turned over to the brigade surgeon, who opened and distributed them to the different hospitals. Never was a provision train more joyously greeted by starving men than was this ample supply of hospital stores by these sick and suffering soldiers.

"On the next day I went forward to the army, reporting myself to Gen. Curtis, introduced by your letters. I found him in an ordinary tent, without furniture, except a stool and a small cross-legged pine table. The floor was covered with straw, and a roll of blankets constituted his bedding. Being invited, I dined with him upon plain army fare. I then proceeded to Gen. Davis' position, within one and a half miles of Elk Horn Tavern, where the heaviest fighting was done. I visited the battle-ground, and was filled with astonishment when I saw the strength of the positions out of which our gallant little army had driven the great force opposed to it. Meeting two rebel surgeons one of them said: 'We are Texans; our army has treated us shamefully; they stampeded, and left us here with our sick and wounded men, and, I will tell you, sir, that for two days we had nothing to give our poor fellows but parched corn and water. Every federal officer and man has treated us like gentlemen, and Gen. Curtis told me that so long as he had a loaf of bread, we should have half it.' This was the field where McCulloch and McIntosh were killed while endeavoring to flank the Peoria battery.

"I visited with these surgeons the hospitals at Pineville. No provision whatever had been made by Price, and our scanty supplies had been shared with them. For twenty-five miles around every house was a rebel hospital. We also had three federal hospitals at Pineville, but not to exceed forty patients. At this point there was a total absence of stimulants, and men were dying for want of them. In one place are forty graves of the Iowa Third Cavalry. All the dead of both armies were buried.

"On my return I called on Gen. Curtis at Keitsville, and promised to urge forward the remaining supplies, which would be sufficient to meet all immediate wants. They were duly forwarded, and reached the command in good time. At Cassville I found that Dr. McGugin, of Iowa, who had been working very faithfully among our suffering men, was completely exhausted. At Springfield I found additional supplies, which had been forwarded by your commission. I was assured that they would go forward on the following morning, and they were rolled out to load up before I left. I am fully convinced that no army was (so far as provision for the wounded was concerned,) ever sent into the field in such destitute condition as ours, *except the one that it fought and conquered.* Our preparations were wholly inadequate ; the enemy had, apparently, made none at all.

"The labors of your commission are most highly appreciated by both officers and men. But for the promptness with which your supplies were sent forward, for which you are greatly indebted to the Commanding General, great suffering must have unavoidably occurred. Could the kind and sympathizing men and women of our loyal States, who place these abundant contributions at your command, but see and realize the thrill of joy with which they were received by the suffering ones, who have so bravely and gladly shed their blood to restore to us a united nation, and to vindicate the majesty of our trampled laws, they would rejoice that they had made the slight sacrifice required to achieve so great a good, and seek, I am sure, to enable you to anticipate rather than to supply, such wants in future.

"Many of these poor sufferers have left distant homes and loving friends ; have been accustomed to receive the tenderest cares and the most watchful sympathy during the slightest indisposition. Now they meet death and grievous wounds, and wasting sickness, in a remote, semi-hostile and thinly settled country, surrounded generally by comparative strangers. And this great sacrifice is most cheerfully made. No word of repining or regret did I hear, but everywhere our gallant men were sustained by an abiding faith that they had suffered and would die, if need be, in a most just and righteous cause."

Mr. Plattenburg's efficiency and usefulness were so satisfactory to the commission, that he was employed from that time as an agent to continue with the Army of the South-west, which he did till the spring of 1863, accompanying it through all its toilsome march from Cassville to Forsyth, returning to St. Louis for sanitary stores, going back to it again overland, and arriving with it at Helena on the following July.

In March, 1863, he proceeded to the vicinity of Vicksburg, with the army of Gen. Grant, remained there in charge of a sanitary boat loaded with stores, and, with his assistants, distributed to the army during the seige of Vicksburg, and after its capture, until the Fall of 1863, when he was sent to the Army of the Cumberland with Gen. Sherman's 15th army corps, and established an agency at Huntsville, Ala., remaining in charge of it till April, 1864, when he resigned his position to attend to interests of his own. During his two years of faithful service, he gained the esteem of the officers of the army, received many testimonials of his great efficiency and usefulness, and always enjoyed the full confidence and support of the Commission.

In December, 1862, the surgeons of the Army of the South-west united in a testimonial in which they say: "The agent of the Commission, Mr. A. W. Plattenburg has always cheerfully furnished for the use of the sick and the wounded, every thing in his possession. Joining this army just after the battle of Pea Ridge, he came with his abundant stores most providentially, and through all dangers, trials, and vicissitudes he has remained constantly with us, and ever faithful to his mission."

In a letter of Maj. Gen. Curtis, dated March 1st, 1863, he says: "Among the pleasant and grateful recollections of the campaign of the South-west was the arrival of Mr. A. W. Plattenburg, the agent of this noble Commission, just after the battle of Pea Ridge (where the wounded were so unprovided for), with his abundant sanitary stores and supplies of stimulants. In the destitute condition of our hospitals it seemed like a providential interposition in our behalf."

Among the incidents at the battle of Pea Ridge worthy of mention in this connection, were the labors of Mrs. Phelps, who had accompanied her husband, Col. John S. Phelps, with his regiment to the battle-field. While the battle was yet raging, this heroic woman assisted in the care of the wounded; tore up her own garments for bandages, dressed their wounds, cooked food and made soup and broth for them to eat with her own hands, remaining with them as long as there was any thing she could do, and giving not only words but deeds of substantial kindness and sympathy. And wherever the cause of our national Union and its perils shall hereafter be known, "this that this woman hath done shall be remembered as a memorial of her."

CHAPTER IV.

SOLDIERS HOME ESTABLISHED AT ST. LOUIS—PREMIUMS AWARDED TO THE STEWARDS AND WARDMASTERS OF THE BEST HOSPITALS, AND TO THE MOST FAITHFUL NURSES—THE BATTLE OF PITTSBURG LANDING—LARGE NUMBER OF WOUNDED—ADDITIONAL HOSPITAL STEAMERS FURNISHED—VOLUNTEER SURGEONS AND NURSES—ADDITIONAL HOSPITALS FITTED UP AT SAINT LOUIS—DEMAND FOR SURGEONS—NUMBER OF SICK AND WOUNDED IN THE ST. LOUIS HOSPITALS—REPORT OF THE COMMISSION.

On the 13th of March, 1862, a Soldier's Home for discharged and furloughed soldiers passing through the city, was established by the Western Commission, at 29 South Fourth Street, St. Louis, capable of accommodating from fifty to one hundred soldiers daily. It was placed in charge of Rev. Charles Peabody as Superintendent, with Miss A. L. Ostram for Matron, and has afforded many a poor, penniless, and invalid soldier food and lodgings, saved others from the sharpers that lie in wait to impose on the unwary, from exorbitant hotel charges, and from the bad associations and influences of the lower class of hotels ; it has been an asylum to many who left the hospitals to go home, not yet fully recovered—some of them returning to their families to die—where on their way they could enjoy a few days of quiet rest, have the aid of the Superintendent in getting their pay and bounty, and the kind attentions of the matron to nurse them and bind up their wounds.

During the first year of its existence, the Soldiers' Home at St. Louis entertained with meals and lodgings, twelve thousand four hundred and ten (12,410) soldier guests, most of them invalids partially restored to health, passing on furlough to their homes, or returning to their regiments.

During its second year to March 12th, 1864, it has entertained eight thousand four hundred and thirty-six (8,436) enlisted men, making a total of twenty thousand eight hundred and forty-six (20,846) soldiers who have enjoyed the hospitality of this Home in a period of two years. And yet compared with four others afterwards established by the Commission at Columbus, Ky., Memphis, Tenn., Helena, Ark., and Vicksburg, Mississippi, the average number entertained has been much less than at those places. This has been partly owing to its smaller accommodations and partly to its greater distance from the seat of war, as our armies obtained possession of the States bordering on the Mississippi River.

Of the 20,846 soldiers who have been the guests of this Home 5,576 have been from Illinois, 4,615 from Iowa, 4,520 from Missouri, 1,795 from Wisconsin, 1,221 from Indiana, 420 from Michigan, 668 from Ohio, 342 from Minnesota, 136 from Kentucky, 359 from Kansas, 82 from Arkansas, 64 from the Marine Brigade, 111 from the U. S. Regulars, 73 from Nebraska, 576 from other States, and 288 from the Invalid Corps.

The number of meals furnished to soldiers for the two years ending March 12th, 1864, was eighty-five thousand nine hundred and ninety-two (85,992), and the number of lodgings for the same period was twenty-four thousand two hundred and ninety, (24,290). In no case has any charge been made to any of the guests. Besides these, many near relatives, fathers, mothers, and wives of sick or furloughed soldiers, accompanying them, have received the hospitality of the Home, of which no account has been made.

The expense incurred by the Commission in maintaining this institution is about $3,000 a year, and the value of the rations and fuel furnished by the Government is about $2,000 more.

The conduct of the soldiers while staying at the Home has generally been respectful, and such as would become good citizens. The hospitality and kind attention given have been almost uniformly received with gratitude. Many on leaving have come to the office and expressed their thanks to the superintendent, and often, although informed that every thing they had received was freely given, have insisted on bestowing something from their hard earnings to help sustain the institution. On being shown to their rooms at night it has been common to hear such expressions as these: "Oh, Jim, see here, this is a nice fat pillow, as sure as you are born, the first I have seen for six months," to which another would reply, "Yes, Sam, these are pillows, sure enough, and this is a clean soft bed. I tell you what, *this makes me think of home.*"

On Thanksgiving and Christmas and New-Year's days it has been customary to provide some fowls and other extras; and at all times, butter, vegetables, milk, dried and canned fruits and tomatoes have been furnished, in addition to the army ration. Very often expressions are heard at the table, or after meals, indicating the grateful appreciation of the soldier, who has been for months confined to hard bread, salt meat, and coffee, without milk, on finding so wholesome and palatable a change of diet. "Well," says one, "I haven't had so good a meal for two years." "Yes," answers another, "this is pretty good fare; if we could only have such all the time we'd get along first rate. But I expect Uncle Sam does the best he can for us. It's hard getting anything down among them Rebs. The sooner we can clean them out and come home the better."

A reading room is provided at this as well as the other Homes, containing several hundred volumes, and the daily papers and several religious journals are also furnished, so that the soldier is able to pass his time pleasantly and profitably during his short stay. He is thus kept from a desire to roam through the city in search of amusement, and goes on his way refreshed in body and mind.

In the winter of 1863, Miss Ostram, the first matron, after nearly a year of faithful service, was transferred to the Home at Memphis, and the situation remained vacant, for a considerable period, during which Mr. John Gibbon acted as clerk and steward, which position he filled with great fidelity. On his retiring, about six months ago, it became necessary to fill the situation of matron, when Mrs. J. E. Rice, now performing the duties with satisfaction, was appointed,

The institution has been conducted with eminent success by Mr. Peabody, the Superintendent, who has shown great executive ability in its management, whose courtesy and kindness to the soldier have given him a place in their grateful remembrance, and whose intercourse with the military authorities, and the members of the commission, has always been such as to win their esteem and confidence.

In his last annual report to the Commission (March 12th, 1864) Mr. Peabody very justly remarks upon the benefits to the country arising from sanitary labors, and from such institutions as the Soldiers' Home:

"Observing from the position I have occupied, the wrecks left behind the wake of armies, the conviction forces itself upon me that the labors of the Sanitary Commission, by the immense supplemental aid it has rendered in furnishing sanitary supplies and establishing Soldiers' Homes, have contributed not a little to saving men for the service, as well as rescuing them from death. In prosecuting their wars the ancients had no hospital trains or medical staff in attendance on their armies. In their military movements the sick and wounded soldiers were left behind to die. In these times, and in our unhappy struggle with a giant rebellion, the soldiers are tenderly cared for, not only by the medical department of the army, but by thousands of patriotic hands, working systematically, through thoroughly organized channels, which often reach far beyond the routine of the service. The future historian of this great struggle will be able to show that the very small per cent of loss among our armies, as compared with that of modern European wars is to be attributed largely to what the people themselves have done through organized voluntary labors in behalf of the soldiers.

"Having aided, under your auspices, in the organization of the Soldiers' Home, established in this city, and watched over it daily for two years, I cannot but express the conviction that for the amount of money expended, this enterprise has brought back in substantial and lasting benefits to the soldiers quite as much as any of the noble undertakings in which your Commission has engaged. It has cheered the disheartened soldier in his toilsome duties. It has saved multitudes from imposition and exactions, and has aided them in securing prompt attention to their just rights. By the substantial comforts and kind attentions which it has afforded it has served to impress on the minds of those who fight our battles the fact that their toils are remembered and their heroic efforts appreciated. Standing in the face of death on the bloody field the recollection of such kind hospitality and attention has served to strengthen their arms and exalt their courage in the deadly conflict. By lending a helping hand to the weak and faltering as they return homewards from their exposures, it has served to assure their friends and the loyal public that the opinion, too current through the land, that the common soldier is always trod upon and abused, is a mistake. It has afforded kind nursing to hundreds of sick and suffering, and by a little care and attention, has saved many valuable lives. It has also afforded the opportunity of impressing moral and religious truth on the minds of the soldiers, and of ministering consolation to some who were just entering upon their last great conflict. In view of the good it has already accomplished, and its capacity for future usefulness to the soldiers and the service, it is warmly commended to your special consideration."

In the early part of April, 1862, the Western Sanitary Commission, wishing to encourage and stimulate a patriotic emulation among the stewards, ward masters, and nurses in the hospitals to excel in their several spheres of duty, and thereby promote the welfare of the sick and wounded, by securing the best possible attention, and the most favorable conditions for recovery, offered a series of premiums as follows, to be paid in gold on the 4th day of the following July:

1. To the head steward of whichever one of the large hospitals

shall have been kept in the best condition, all things considered, and in which the comfort of the patients shall have been uniformly best cared for, in every way, through a term of three months, the sum of TWENTY-FIVE DOLLARS.

2. To the head steward of the best of the smaller hospitals, as above estimated, the sum of FIFTEEN DOLLARS.

3. To the best assistant steward in every large hospital, who shall be the most punctual, attentive and diligent in the performance of his duties, the sum of TEN DOLLARS.

4. To the best assistant steward, estimated as above, in all the small hospitals, the sum ot EIGHT DOLLARS.

5. To the best ward master in each of the large hospitals, whose ward shall have been uniformly kept in the best and most perfect order, as to cleanliness of beds and bedding, the comfort of the patients, and in all other respects, the sum of TEN DOLLARS.

6. To the best ward master in each of the small hospitals, estimated as above, the sum of EIGHT DOLLARS.

7. To the best twenty nurses, in all the hospitals, who shall remain in service through the three months, and who shall prove themselves the most kind, faithful and attentive, in the discharge of all their duties to the sick, FIVE DOLLARS EACH.

8. To the best culinary department, in all the hospitals—that is, for the best and cleanest kitchen, the best and most wholesome cookery, with the smallest waste, the sum of TWENTY-FIVE DOLLARS, the same to be divided between the head cook and assistants, in the hospital to which the prize shall be awarded, in such proportions as may seem just.

9. To the second best kitchen, etc., estimated as above, the sum of FIFTEEN DOLLARS.

10. To every female nurse who shall remain in the service for three months, and shall have given full satisfaction, a certificate shall be awarded, with special vote of thanks.

11. To the best hospital, all things considered, a public expression of thanks shall be given, with the approval of the Medical Director and of the General commanding.

To secure the just award of these premiums and testimonials, the Sanitary Commission will make weekly, or more frequent, visits of inspection to every hospital under direction of the Head Surgeon, and in consultatlon with him, and a careful record of each visit and its results will be kept.

A monthly inspection will also be made, with the same view, by order of the General commanding.

In offering these premiums, the "Western Sanitary Commission" are actuated by a desire to assist the medical staff in making the military hospitals of the "Department of the Mississippi," the most perfect in the United States.

This undertaking had the sanction of the Commanding General of the Department, and of the Medical Director, and its influence was highly beneficial in stimulating the best endeavors of those who filled the stewardships in the hospitals, and had the immediate care of the sick and wounded—not so much for the sake of the pecuniary rewards as from the consciousness that their labors were carefully noticed and appreciated, which gave an additional spur to their humane interest in the soldier, and excited a laudable and proper ambition to receive the award of well doing.

The persons to whom these awards were finally made were as follows: To Mr. George Thomas, chief steward of the Fifth Street Hospital, $25; to Mr. Kleuber, chief steward of Camp Benton Hospital, $15; to Mr. Matthews, assistant steward in the Fifth Street Hospital, $10; to Messrs. James McCrea, George Miran, and Henry Crawshaw, ward masters in the Fifth Street Hospital each $10; to Messrs. Loar, Henry Sanders, and James Larkin, nurses in the Fifth Street Hospital, and to Mr. Charles Tising, nurse in the Good Samaritan Hospital, $5; to the chief cook and assistants in the culinary department of the New House of Refuge Hospital, $25; to the chief cook and assistants in the culinary department of the Camp Benton Hospital, $15; and to the following female nurses, with certificates and a vote of thanks, $5 each: Mrs. Morris, Mrs. Ballard, Mrs. Parker, Mrs. Gibson, Mrs. Aldrich, Mrs. Houghton, Mrs. Brooks, Mrs. Ferris, Mrs. Campbell, Mrs. Plummer, Miss McNair, Mrs. Colfax, Mrs. Barton, Miss Johnson, Miss Clark, Miss Cullom, Miss Ostram, Mrs. Starr, Mrs. Freeman.

On the 6th and 7th of April, 1862, occurred the great battle of Pittsburg Landing, on the Tennessee river, between the Union forces under General Grant, and the rebel forces under General A. S. Johnson and General Beauregard. In this battle, the loss to the Union army was 1,735 killed, and 7,882 wounded; and to the rebels, 1,728 killed, and 8,012 wounded, many of whom fell into our hands.

The news of this terrible battle was brought to St. Louis by telegraph, and Maj. Gen. Halleck immediately addressed a note to the Western Sanitary Commission, requesting its co-operation with the medical and quartermaster's departments in sending steamers, properly fitted up, furnished with medical and sanitary supplies, and a requisite force of surgeons, wound-dressers and nurses to take care of the wounded, and return with them to St. Louis; also in fitting up additional hospital accommodations in this city to receive them.

The following note was received from the Chief Quartermaster:

QUARTERMASTER'S DEPARTMENT, OFFICE OF TRANSPORTATION,
St. Louis, April 10th, 1862.

JAS. E. YEATMAN, Esq.,

President Western Sanitary Commission:

DEAR SIR: I have arranged with the owners of the steamers "*Continental*," "*Crescent City*" and "*Imperial*," to remain on or go to the Tennessee river for the relief and use of the sick and wounded. In case you find it necessary or desirable, you will please direct either of these boats to such points as you may deem best for these purposes, and I will settle for the time they are detained in the service, on your certificate. These boats, so taken, are not to be interfered with while in use for hospital purposes.

Respectfully,

LEWIS B. PARSONS,

Capt. and A. Q. M.

The following, of the same date, was also directed to the captain of the steamer "*Empress*," from the same source:

"You will at once proceed to Pittsburg, Tenn., unless otherwise ordered by James E. Yeatman, Esq., President Western Sanitary Commission, who will accompany you on the trip. * * * You will return to this point as soon as you can consistently be discharged from the duty on which you are sent, namely, for 'hospital purposes.'"

The hospital steamer "*City of Louisiana*," arrived on the 9th of April from Pittsburg Landing with three hundred and fifty sick, having left there previous to the battle. On the receipt of the intelligence that a battle had been fought, she returned the next day, to the scene of conflict, with additional sanitary stores.

The steamer "*D. A. January*," which had been purchased by the Government for a hospital steamer, fitted up by the Western Commission, and placed in charge of Surgeon A. H. Hoff, U. S. V., was also sent to Pittsburg Landing. This boat from the date of this battle to the month of August, made eight trips, and conveyed 2,692 patients from ports on the Tennessee and Lower Mississippi rivers to northern hospitals, mostly to the hospitals of Saint Louis. She has been remodeled, in accordance with plans of Surgeon Hoff, and continued in the service, having rendered incalculable benefits, accommodating five hundred patients, and bringing from Vicksburg, Helena, and elsewhere, many thousands of sick and wounded to St. Louis and affording them the best possible treatment on the way.

On the evening of the 10th of April the steamer "*Empress*," being furnished by the Western Sanitary Commission with a complete outfit of medical and sanitary stores, with a corps of surgeons, wound-dressers, and nurses, both for herself and the large and splendid steamer "*Imperial*," (then on the Tennessee river,) started for Pittsburg Landing, in charge of the President of the Commission (Mr. Yeatman), where, on her arrival, the outfit for the "*Imperial*" was transferred to that boat, and all were loaded with the wounded with as much expedition as was possible.

On this expedition there accompanied Mr. Yeatman Drs. Pollak, Grove, Azpell, May, Bixby, and Barnes, Surgeon Grove, U. S. V., taking charge of the "*Imperial*" on arriving at Pittsburg, with the requisite force of assistant surgeons, stewards, wound-dressers, nurses, etc.

A delegation of noble women from St. Louis, members of the Ladies' Union Aid Society, also accompanied this expedition as volunteer nurses, and rendered invaluable service. Among those now remembered who thus gave their timely aid was Mrs. Washington King, Mrs. Foster, Mrs. Perley Child, Mrs. J. E. D. Couzins, Mrs. C. B. Fisk, Mrs. J. Crawshaw, and Miss Patrick.

On the return trip the steamer "*Empress*" was loaded with nine hundred wounded men, her guards, decks, and cabins being filled, and friend and foe alike provided for; for many wounded prisoners fell into our hands on the second day of the battle. The "*Imperial*" also returned loaded in a similar manner, and continued to run for several months as a floating hospital in charge of Surgeon Grove. The "*City of Louisiana*," "*D. A. January*," and the "*Crescent City*," also returned with their cargoes of human lives, and the wounded were received into the hospitals of St. Louis.

The crowded condition of the hospitals and want of room made it necessary that additional hospital accommodations should be immediately provided. The Western Sanitary Commission proceeded at once to procure two large halls in Arnot's and Thornton's and Pierce's buildings on Chesnut and Walnut streets, and furnished them with beds and furniture and sanitary stores, and with the requisite number of nurses, for the accommodation of three hundred and twenty sick and wounded men.

During the midst of these labors Maj. Gen. Halleck telegraphed the Commission from Pittsburg Landing to send twenty surgeons to that place for duty there. Nine were procured and went forward the same day, and afterwards an additional number.

On the first of May the Commission made a report of its labors, from which the following particulars are selected as completing an outline of its history to this date:

There were then fifteen military hospitals in and about St. Louis, affording accommodations for for 5,750 patients, and a reserve was constantly maintained in readiness by the Commission of 250 beds in addition, making a total of 6,000. The number of patients admitted to that date was 19,467, of whom 1,400 had died; 15,717 had been furloughed, discharged, or returned to their regiments, and 3,750 remained. There had been 162 additional deaths on floating hospitals in transit, at McDowell's military prison, the St. Louis Arsenal, and at private houses. The number of patients on hand was unusually small, great numbers having been furloughed, in order to relieve the hospitals, pending the expected battle at Corinth.

The Commission had fitted four floating hospitals, regularly employed for the transportation of the sick and wounded in the Department of the Mississippi, the "*City of Louisiana*," Dr. Wagner, the "*D. A. January*," Dr. Huff, the "*Imperial*," Dr. Grove, and the "*Empress*," Dr. Azpell, all very large and fine steamers, altered and arranged for this purpose. They were capable of transporting two thousand sick or wounded men, and were fully provided with experienced surgeons, assistant surgeons, apothecaries, stewards, dressers, and male and female nurses. They had every convenience that experience could suggest, and were supplied with large reserves of hospital clothing, lint, bandages, delicacies, fruit, &c., that they might be prepared to furnish temporary transports or field hospitals whenever and wherever needed.

As these boats were constantly plying between St. Louis and the immediate vicinity of all probable battle fields, no better method of securing prompt relief wherever needed could have been devised or desired.

The first two of these boats remained permanently in the service, to which others were added at a later period.

The hospital steamer "*City of Memphis*," in charge of Surgeon W. D. Turner, U. S. A., had also been supplied with hospital furniture and stores by the Commission.

There can be no doubt that these floating hospitals have saved hundreds of priceless lives, by transporting the sick and wounded promptly from the field to well regulated hospitals, and by furnishing in transit good surgical attendance and nursing, and comfortable accommodations.

During the eight months the Commission had then existed it had received 985 cases of goods from eighteen States, viz:

State	Cases	State	Cases
Massachusetts	223	New Hampshire	16
Illinois	132	New Jersey	11
Wisconsin	74	Minnesota	10
Rhode Island	69	Indiana	9
Pennsylvania	63	Connecticut	7
Missouri	61	Vermont	6
Iowa	57	Maine	5
New York	51	Delaware	4
Michigan	40	District of Columbia	3
Ohio	12	Not ascertained	137

Besides these, it had also received large contributions in money and goods from the citizens of St. Louis and vicinity, not included in the above statement, for the reason that they had been received in bulk, in many instances by the wagon load, and in thousands of small packages.

The articles distributed by the Commission, to that date, numbered 166,288, including 6,813 blankets, 8,065 sheets, 7,034 pillows, 11,545 pillow-cases, 10,443 towels, 5,249 handkerchiefs, 21,577 shirts, 11,159 pair drawers, 19,519 pair socks, 4,384 pair slippers, 1,841 dressing gowns, 1,032 articles of clothing, 18,196 books and pamphlets, 3,084 pads, 981 bottles of domestic wines, 1,459 cans jelly, 2,340 pounds farina, 1,400 cans fruit, and 25,000 miscellaneous articles, such as mittens, games, crutches, work bags, bed pans, spit cups, picket caps, pin cushions, eye shades, slings, india rubber syringes, isinglass plasters, remedies, etc. In addition to these the Commission purchased large numbers of articles for the complete outfit of the city and floating hospitals, and for armies in the field, embracing air and water beds, washing machines, implements of various kinds, barrels of stimulants, (of better quality and in larger supply than furnished by Government,) of eggs and chickens, cases of oranges and lemons, hundreds of pairs of crutches, invalid chairs of novel construction, bedsteads, cots, mattresses, graduated back-rests, stands or stools for the bedside, sideboards for the proper security and arrangement of medicines, disinfectants, splints, and innumerable other articles. Seventy-four hospitals had then been supplied. The demand from every quarter rapidly increased and the distribution had reached the rate of 17,000 articles per week.

Thus the labors of the Commission were greatly increased, and the work of ministering to the sick and wounded went forward night and day. Another great battle, it was expected, would soon occur at Corinth, and the hopes and anxieties of the loyal people of the country were raised to their highest degree of intensity. But the evacuation of that position by the rebel forces, and their escape under their arrogant and boastful commander, General Beauregard, in the presence of the powerful Union army that was arrayed against them by Maj. Gen. Halleck, now commanding in person, disappointed the public expectation; and, notwithstanding the retreat of the rebels gave us some of the fruits of a decisive victory, yet they were enabled by this movement to get away without any substantial loss, to go and assist in the defense of Richmond, and to transfer the contest to Virginia, where the great battles of the Peninsula followed in the summer of 1862. In the West, it only remained to follow up our naval victories from Island No. 10 to Memphis and Helena, and to hold the ground already gained till another great campaign could be inaugurated in the fall of the same year. It now became necessary to attend to the sick, occasioned by the diseases of camp life, and the malaria of the southern climate, to look after the camps and hospitals in Arkansas and Tennessee, and to continue the supplies to the hospital steamers of the western rivers, and to the general hospitals established at various points from St. Lonis to Helena. The labors of the Commission during the summer of 1862 will form the subject of the next chapter.

CHAPTER V.

LETTER OF THE COMMISSION TO THE SURGEON-GENERAL—SCOLLAY'S DEODORIZING BURIAL CASE—CAPTURE OF FORT PILLOW AND MEMPHIS—OPENING OF THE MISSISSIPPI RIVER TO VICKSBURG—FITTING OUT THE NAVAL HOSPITAL BOAT "RED ROVER"—ARRIVAL OF GEN. CURTIS' ARMY AT HELENA—ITS DESTITUTE CONDITION—SICKNESS OF THE ARMY AT HELENA—SANITARY DEPOT ESTABLISHED THERE—OVERTON HOSPITAL AT MEMPHIS—SICK FROM THE ARMY IN TENNESSEE—HOSPITALS AND REGIMENTS SUPPLIED—THE NAVY—LETTER FROM COMMODORE DAVIS—AN EARNEST APPEAL FROM THE COMMISSION—GENEROUS RESPONSE FROM NEW ENGLAND.

THE intimate connection of the Western Sanitary Commission with the hospitals of St. Louis, and of the Department of the Mississippi, and the frequent inspections made by its members, had given opportunity to observe defects, and to suggest remedies. Among the evils that arrested attention was that of insufficient space and air to each patient, many of the hospitals being too much crowded, hindering and preventing the recovery of the sick, especially in cases of typhoid fever, erysipelas, and badly wounded men.

On the 8th of May, the Commission addressed the following communication to the Surgeon-General of the U. S. Army, at Washington:

SAINT LOUIS, *May 8th*, 1862.

DR. WM. A. HAMMOND,

Surgeon-General U. S. A.:

SIR: The Western Sanitary Commission of the Department of the Mississippi, most respectfully suggest the importance and necessity of some rule or law regulating the amount of space allowed to every patient in hospital. In the absence of such a rule great mistakes are made, and in many hospitals, otherwise well conducted, the beds are so crowded together, and the number of cubic feet of air to each patient is so inadequate, that fatal consequences result.

The members of the Commission having had large opportunities of observation, confidently express the opinion that not more than half the space necessary for the successful treatment of the sick, and especially of the wounded men, is usually allowed in the general and post hospitals.

By actual measurement they find that the average of square feet on the floor, allowed in some of the best hospitals even, for typhoid and erysipelas and badly wounded patients is only forty or fifty feet per bed, and sometimes less ; and of cubic feet of air only three hundred and fifty to eight hundred feet, little regard being paid to the height of the rooms occupied.

They believe that no degree of cleanliness or care, or of professional skill can remove the evil effects of such over crowding, and that there is no way of preventing its continuance except by positive regulation.

In making these suggestions the Commission has no design of complaint. The hospitals of this department are almost all well conducted and the patients well and skillfully treated, and the surgeons would undoubtedly be glad to have authority to correct the evils referred to. The near approach of warm weather makes the subject one of urgent importance, and it has already become of painful interest to the Commission, during a recent thorough inspection of hospitals, containing over four thousand sick and wounded men, many of whom are seriously suffering from the causes named.

The Commission is of the opinion that the minimum space in well ventilated hospitals should be six hundred and forty cubic feet for each bed, and for typhoid cases, erysipelas, and severely wounded men, not less than twelve hundred feet. Larger space would be desirable, but practical difficulties of various kinds frequently occur to make it unattainable consistently with the general interests of the service.

The Commission therefore respectfully and earnestly submit this matter to the consideration of the Surgeon General, and have the honor to remain,

His obedient servants,

JAMES E. YEATMAN,
C. S. GREELEY,
J. B. JOHNSON,
GEORGE PARTRIDGE,
WM. G. ELIOT.

The subject submitted to the Surgeon General in this letter received his favorable consideration, and in the hospitals afterwards established a sufficient and specified number of cubic feet of air was allowed to each bed. In the case of the Lawson Hospital on Broadway, the regulation has been carried out very thoroughly, and the prescribed number of cubic feet of air allowed to the beds, in the several wards, is lettered over the entrance ; the ward having the largest space containing 778 cubic feet to a bed, and the lowest allowance in any ward being 606 cubic feet to a bed.

In the spring of this year a most useful invention was brought to the attention ot the Western Commission, designed to afford a safer, cheaper, and better method of preserving the remains of deceased persons without burial, for transportation to friends at a distance, an object greatly desired by those having relations killed in battle, or dying in the military hospitals. The invention bore the name of "Dr. Scollay's Deodorizing Coffin or Burial Case," and was submitted to a series of experiments before a committee of the Commission, consisting of Drs. S. Pollak, Chas. A. Pope, and J. B. Johnson, Rev. M. Schuyler, D. D., and R. R. Hazard, Jr., Esq.

The burial case is thus described in the report of this committee: "Taking the ordinary wooden coffin he [Dr. Scollay] has so improved it as to make it in all respects equal, and in many superior, to the iron, or any other case now in use. The coffin is made effectually air-tight by a peculiar match joint and a coating of cement, which not only renders it impervious to air and fluid under ordinary pressure, but must greatly preserve the wood from decay. To preserve the coffin from rupture under the extraordinary pressure of the gases arising from decomposition, and to render the escape of such gases impossible, unless *deodorized,* a provision is made which constitutes the principal feature of the improvement. This consists of a deodorizing chamber, placed inside, at the foot of the coffin, of such size and so arranged as not to increase its bulk or alter its form. * * * This chamber is so arranged and divided that the escaping gases pass freely through apertures into the lower division, and thence into the middle apartment, which is filled with a *deodorizing chemical compound.* Through this they pass into the upper apartment, which is furnished with a self-adjusting valve, which yields to a moderate pressure and permits their escape."

The experiments of the committee proved that bodies may be preserved in these burial cases without becoming offensive for many months, not the slightest smell being perceived, even in the warmest weather—in one case after 150 days. In another instance, in which antiseptic agents were used before encasing, it was observed, after nearly two months, that decomposition had been very slight, and the body was quite natural in its appearance, and in a recognizable condition.

The committee concluded their report as follows: "The cases can be furnished at a trifling advance upon the ordinary wooden coffin in general use. They are light for handling and transportation, not liable to explosion, and it is reasonable to believe from the tests already presented that bodies may be kept in them from thirty to fifty days, and perhaps longer, without becoming offensive, and the necessity of immediate burial and a disagreeable interment be avoided."

The subsequent use of these deodorizing coffins, by Mr. Smithers, government undertaker of this city, has more than established the correctness of the foregoing conclusions. The deodorizing coffin was afterwards sent to Washington, and after a series of experiments there, was approved by the Surgeon General, and Mr. Smithers was contracted with by Colonel Myers, A. Q. M., at St. Louis, to use it in the burial of all soldiers from the hospitals of this city, so that they might afterwards be more conveniently removed by their friends. But the Quartermaster General at Washington disapproved the contract, and it was never carried into effect.

On the 12th of April the gunboats of the Mississippi Naval Squadron left New Madrid, just below Island No. 10, and proceeded down the river to Fort Pillow in Tennessee. An attack was made on the fort the next day, but was not attended with immediate success. On the 4th of May a severe naval battle occurred at this point between our gunboats and a Confederate ram and gunboats from below, who came up and commenced the attack, in the hope of destroying or capturing our naval force, including the mortar boats. The result of the engagement was disastrous to the rebels, one of their boats having been sunk and two others blown up, while their whole fleet was crippled, and withdrew down the river. One of our boats, the "Cincinnati," was disabled, and four of her crew wounded.

On the 4th of June Forts Pillow and Randolph were evacuated by the Confederates, and on the 5th our fleet arrived at Memphis, consisting of the gunboats Benton, Cairo, Carondelet, Louisville, and St. Louis, and the four rams Monarch, Lancaster, No. 3, and the Queen of the West. On the 6th a great naval battle ensued, the Confederates bringing into the engagement the gunboats Beauregard, Little Rebel, General Price, General Bragg, General Lovell, General Van Dorn, Jeff. Thompson, and the Sumpter. The scene of the battle was in front of the city, viewed by thousands of spectators, and the result of an hour's fighting was the destruction of the entire Confederate fleet, which was either sunk, or run ashore, except the General Van Dorn, a swift vessel, which escaped down the river. By this victory Memphis was captured, and the Mississippi river opened as far down as Vicksburg, against which some naval operations were undertaken, and an attempt made to change the current of the river by a canal, which were afterwards abandoned.

By these events a new field of operations was opened to the Western Sanitary Commission. The naval squadron had now its own sick and wounded to be provided for, and general hospitals were immediately established at Memphis and Jackson, Tenn., and at Helena, Ark.

At a meeting of the Commission held the 22d of May, the President reported that Capt. Wise of the gunboat flotilla had proposed that the steamer "*Red Rover*," a fine large boat, captured from the enemy at Island No. 10, should be fitted up by the Commission, as a floating hospital, for the Mississippi Naval Squadron, towards which he would furnish $2000, of the expense.

She was accordingly remodeled in her cabin arrangements, and a complete outfit of beds, bedding, furniture, sanitary stores, medical dispensary, etc., supplied by the Commission, the services of surgeons, an apothecary, steward and nurses were engaged, and the boat placed in charge of Dr. Geo. H. Bixby, surgeon, and Dr. Hopkins, assistant surgeon, two thoroughly educated and skillful young physicians who were sent out from Boston by that philanthropist and friend of the soldier, James M. Barnard. Their services were so highly appreciated that, in a few months, they received the unsolicited honor of a regular commission in the U. S. Navy as assistant surgeons. Dr. Bixby has continued in charge of the "*Red Rover*" to the present date, and Dr. Hopkins also remains in the service, in which they have both acquired a high reputation and are greatly esteemed. The expense incurred by the Commission out of its own funds, in fitting up this boat, was $3,500, which was done with the greatest satisfaction for the brave men who had fought so nobly, and gained so many victories on our western waters.

On the 10th of July the Army of the South-west under Maj. Gen. Curtis, arrived at Helena in a condition of great destitution. The toilsome march from Batesville under the intense heats of summer, the want of provisions, the difficulty of finding water to drink, and what was procured being often muddy and stagnant, caused much sickness to follow the severe privation of the troops on that terrible march, in which the heroes of Pea Ridge fought their way through to a new base of supplies and a river communication with St. Louis.

In midsummer, this army of ten thousand men pitched their tents on the bottom lands of the Mississippi, around, above and below Helena, and on the hill-sides and in the woods lying back of the town, and a more unhealthy location could scarcely have been found. But it was the only situation that could be occupied on the west side of the Mississippi below Memphis; its communication with Little Rock by the Clarendon road, its commercial advantages, its excellent houses, its convenience for storage of commissary and ordnance stores all made it important that it should be held as a military post.

The regiments suddenly changing their mode of life from the rugged and toilsome marches to which they had been accustomed, to one of comparative inactivity, using water from the Mississippi, or from the poor springs and rivulets that were found along the margin of the stagnant cypress swamps that lie back of Helena, it was not surprising that many of these stalwart men were soon brought down with bilious, remittent, intermittent and typhoid fevers, and with diarrhea, so that during the autumn months, the regimental hospitals were filled, and the five churches of the town, with one exception, were all converted into hospitals.

Mr. Plattenburg, the agent of the Commission, who had continued with this army from Pea Ridge through all its lengthy march over the Ozark Mountains and through the plains and bottom lands of Arkansas, by a circuitous route of nearly eight hundred miles, now opened a depot at Helena, and received a full supply of sanitary stores, which he dispensed liberally to the regimental surgeons for their sick; and to all the troops many articles of comfort were given, such as towels, handkerchiefs, combs, canned fruits, and vegetables, potatoes, onions, &c. These gifts were received with the strongest expressions of gratitude, after so much destitution, hardship and suffering, and did much to prevent disease and alleviate distress.

At Memphis one of the largest and finest buildings in the city, intended orignally for a hotel, was taken for hospital purposes, and called "The Overton Hospital." To Surgeon Derby, who was placed in charge of it, frequent shipments of sanitary stores were sent to meet the wants of the sick from the armies of Tennessee.

At St. Louis the work of friendly inspection and oversight of hospitals went on through the summer and autumn of 1862, and large supplies of sanitary goods were sent to the hospitals and regiments, hospital steamers and gunboats, throughout the Departments of Missouri, the Tennessee, and the Mississippi.

The gunboats and naval hospital boat of the Mississippi squadron had also been kept liberally supplied during this year. In September, the following letter was received from Commodore Davis, showing his high appreciation of the services rendered by the Commission:

FLAGSHIP EASTPORT,
HELENA, September 18, 1862.

SIR: The present season is about drawing to a close, and upon the recommendation of Dr. Bixby, I have sent the hospital steamer Red Rover to St. Louis, to be properly fitted up for the winter.

I cannot let her return to your vicinity without expressing, in behalf of myself and the officers and crews of the vessels under my command, our heartfelt and grateful acknowledgments for your uniform kindness and attention to the wants of the sick of the squadron.

I beg you to believe that your benevolent labors in our behalf have been fully appreciated.

I have the honor to be, with the utmost respect,

Your obedient servant and friend,

(Signed,) C. H. DAVIS,

Commodore Commanding Western Flotilla.

JAMES E. YEATMAN, ESQ.,

President Western Santary Commission.

Letters were also received from Acting Rear Admiral David D. Porter, and from the Surgeon in Chief of the Naval Flotilla, W. Whelan, in October, expressive of similar sentiments, and acknowledging the receipt of sanitary stores.

The resources of the Commission at this time had become very much reduced. The great battles in Virginia and Maryland, between Generals McClellan and Lee, commencing on the Peninsula, in May, continued before Richmond, and ending at Antietam, in November, had caused all voluntary contributions from New England and the Middle States, to flow in that direction, and the Western Commission had for months been thrown on its own resources and the aid of the citizens of St. Louis. Notwithstanding this diminution of its resources, the Western Commission also responded to the call of the Surgeon General, and forwarded fifty boxes containing supplies of lint, bandages, &c., to Washington.

It now became necessary, however, to issue an earnest appeal for a replenishment of its stores, from which an extract is here given, showing its wants, the extent of its opportunities, and the work to be done.

"The demands upon this Commission are as great as at any previous time, and the field of its labors is daily enlarged. An army of not less than one hundred and fifty thousand men, in Tennessee, Kentucky, Arkansas and Missouri, and the gunboat flotilla, looks to St. Louis for nearly all its sanitary supplies, and must continue to do so through the war, as the most convenient and accessible place at all seasons of the year. Heretofore the Commission has been able to meet all requisitions. It has never refused to send liberally and promptly to any point, whatever has been needed to alleviate suffering and to cure or prevent sickness.

"In Missouri, Tennessee and Arkansas, the demand for all kinds of hospital supplies is great, and increasing, for a war of unprecedented malignancy has begun to be waged, and exposures of our brave men both to disease and wounds are fearfully great. Those who are at a distance from the scene of action, can have no adequate idea of the privations and hardships of the service, or of the number of those broken down by it. The casualties of the battle-field are but a small item in the estimate. Forced marches, the murderous rifle of an unseen and skulking enemy, who knows the work of the assassin better than that of the soldier, fill our hospitals, and thin our ranks. To such risks are our sons and kindred exposed from day to day, in defense of the country which we all love so well. Has money any value greater than to supply their need? Ought we to become niggardly in gifts, or weary of work in such a cause? Can the women of America enjoy or *endure* the luxury of peaceful homes, except on condition of giving the labor of their hands and the prayers of their hearts to those who are defending them at such a cost?

* * * * * * * * *

"This appeal is most earnestly and affectionately made to all loyal and humane persons in the Union. They have already done much, but redoubled efforts in all departments of the war must now be made. The 600,000 new recruits will not be without their sick and wounded, and many a hard battle must yet be fought. Let the rich give of their abundance. Let the poor spare all they can.

"Especially we appeal to LOYAL WOMEN, wherever they may be. They are the true "Home Guards" of the nation—the ministering angels to sickness and suffering. Without them Sanitary Commissions can do but a small part of their work, and upon their efficient assistance we principally depend."

This appeal was nobly responded to from New England, Boston alone sending $9,000 at this time, and a few months later contributing $50,000 more, for sanitary purposes in the western armies. One noble and patriotic woman in that city, Mrs. Thomas Lamb, has appropriated a room in her own house for the reception of sanitary goods, for the western soldiers, letting it be known to her friends, and the result has been that she has packed and forwarded to this Commission of her own and their contributions, over one hundred boxes of hospital supplies, garments, etc., besides generous sums of money, the boxes ranging in value from $150 to $200 each. Other humane and patriotic friends, among them Messrs. James M. Barnard and R. C. Greenleaf, have also labored most indefatigably in the same way, and endeared themselves forever to all who knew of their noble services to the soldiers in the armies of the west. When it is remembered that Massachusetts has had her own sons, mainly in the armies of the Potomac, and in the Department of the South and of the Gulf, and that without neglecting her duty to them, she has made the most generous donations of any other State to our western troops, no one can fail to appreciate so noble an example of disinterested patriotism and benevolence.

CHAPTER VI.

Army of the Frontier—Agent sent to Springfield, Mo., with Stores—Battles at Cross Hollows, Cane Hill, and Prairie Grove—Arrival of Rev. Mr. Newell at Fayetteville with Ambulances and Sanitary Goods—His useful services—His Death at a later period—Notice of his Character—Flying Hospitals—Additional Hospitals at St. Louis—The Marine, Jefferson Barracks and Lawson Hospitals—The diminishing percentage of Deaths—The hopeful condition of the Armies of the Union—The Sympathy of the People with the Soldiers—Prospects of Ultimate Victory.

In the Fall of 1862 Brig. Gen. Schofield took command of the Army of the Frontier, beyond Springfield, Mo., and on leaving St. Louis, expressed the desire that the Commission would forward a full supply of sanitary stores to that post. The suggestion was favorably regarded and acted upon, and an agent, Mr. J. E. Tefft, sent forward, furnished with every thing necessary as a supplement to the medical stores allowed to the surgeons in the field.

Many supplies had been previously sent to Surgeon Melcher, Medical Director at Springfield, and the additions now made were forwarded in view of the probability of more active hostilities between the Union and rebel forces of the south-west.

This anticipation proved to be well founded. Towards the end of October, in the north-west part of Arkansas, near the old battle-field of Pea Ridge, at Cross Hollows, Gen. Herron had a severe engagement with the enemy; and again on the 28th of November, Gen. Blunt made an attack on Gen. Marmaduke, with about eight thousand men, at Cane Hill, forty-five miles north of Van Buren, in which the rebels were defeated, and retreated to that place. Again, on the 7th of December, the combined Confederate forces, under the command of Gen. Hindman, estimated at fifteen thousand men, attempted to cut off the reinforcements of Gen. Blunt, ten miles south of Fayetteville, and made an attack on Gen. Herron before he had formed a junction with Gen. Blunt. Gen. Herron's forces, however, held their ground until Gen. Blunt, who was informed of the movement, came upon the rear of the rebel army, at Crawford's Prairie, when there occurred what has since been called the battle of Prairie Grove, in which the rebels were defeated, the loss in killed and wounded on both sides being very great.

The wounded from this battle were removed to Fayetteville, and public buildings and private houses were taken for hospitals; but there was a great deficiency of means to take proper care of the men, the town and the country around it having been greatly impoverished by the war, and the inhabitants being of the poorest class. There was no adequate supply of bandages, lint, bedding, stimulants, nor means of fitting up the empty houses and making them comfortable, nor of cooking food.

Previous to this battle the Commission had sent forward Rev. Frederick R. Newell to Springfield, to take the place of Mr. Tefft, with two ambulances and additional stores, and on hearing of this battle he proceeded on from Springfield to Fayetteville. His arrival was most timely, and, with an earnest devotion to duty, he turned over every thing he had to Surgeon Ira Russell, U. S. V., in charge, and Assistant Surgeon Carpenter, and went to work himself at whatever his hands could find to do. For a time he acted as carpenter, ambulance driver, nurse, wound-dresser, and general worker, and in the report afterwards made by the Surgeons, his services were spoken of in the highest terms of commendation.

In the report of Surgeon Russell, he said: "My thanks are due to the Western Sanitary Commission for the valuable aid rendered to the wounded from the battle of Prairie Grove, by its agent, Mr. F. R. Newell." In Dr. Carpenter's report he said: "Mr. Newell's sanitary stores were a perfect God-send to our poor fellows, many of whom had lost nearly all their clothing on the battle field. He made a judicious distribution of his shirts, drawers, and other articles, among the most needy. He also placed at our disposal two ambulances, without which we could hardly have carried on the hospital. Enough cannot be said of an institution which performs such deeds."

As Mr. Newell has since been removed from his earthly labors to the heavenly life, it is proper that some further mention should here be made of him. After the battle of Prairie Grove he continued for several months to act as the agent of the Western Commission at Springfield, Mo., and in May, 1863, returned to St. Louis, where he was, soon after, elected chaplain of the 1st Missouri State Militia, and assigned, by an order of Maj. Gen. Schofield, to the duty of superintendent of freedmen in this city. For several months he attended to this work in a faithful and conscientious manner, interrupted occasionally by illness, when, on the 8th of January, 1864, after a severe attack of inflammatory rheumatism, he died suddenly, at Benton Barracks, at his post.

As a friend of the poor freedmen and their families, as a Christian minister and a citizen, as a man of amiable, forbearing, and Christlike spirit, he will be long remembered by those who were associated with him in his labors, and who knew of his fidelity to the cause of his Divine Master.

During the fall of 1863 the idea originated in the Western Sanitary Commission of a Flying Hospital, to accompany the army in the field, prepared for the emergencies of battle, with the means of immediately providing for wounded men. The President of the Commission was authorized to fit out three ambulances, with hospital and shelter tents, cots, bedding, towels, sanitary stores, food, liquors, bandages, lint, sponges, vessels for supplying the wounded with water and stimulants, the whole to be in charge of a competent person, with a corps of male nurses and wound-dressers in attendance, to accompany the army, to be under the direction of the medical director, and ready at all times to assist the surgeons when required. Two pannier mules were also to accompany each ambulance, with straps and fixtures, by which kegs of water and stimulants, and other articles of immediate utility on the battle field, could be carried on their backs, and be at hand when most needed. The plan was submitted to Assistant Surgeon General Wood, and met with his entire approbation.

The first of these Flying Hospitals was fitted up for Gen. Grant's army, then at Corinth, Miss., and a letter, endorsed by the Assistant Surgeon General, was addressed to Maj. Gen. Grant, asking permission for it to accompany his movements. The Flying Hospital went forward to Lagrange, Tennessee, where the Medical Director, Surgeon Wirtz, refused his sanction, and would not permit it to go any further. The letter to Gen. Grant probably never reached him, as no answer was ever received, and the opposition of his chief surgeon defeated an enterprize which was, in every respect, practicable and unobjectionable, having for its object the better care and prompt relief of our wounded soldiers on the field of battle. Some prejudice against Sanitary Commissions, or too great a readiness to regard their proffered assistance as an interference with official dignity and routine, or some failure of military etiquette, are supposed to have stood in the way of this beneficent project. The mules and ambulances were afterwards returned to the Soldiers' Homes at Columbus and Memphis, where they did good service ; the stores were distributed to the sick, and the nurses and wound-dressers performed valuable services in the hospitals at Lagrange and elsewhere.

The outfit of Rev. Mr. Newell, as an agent of the Commission with Gen. Schofield's army, with his ambulances and stores, was similar in its character, and proved exceedingly useful, after the battle of Prairie Grove, though not arriving in time to be present at the battle.

The difficulty of procuring the necessary sanction, and co-operation of the regular army surgeons to such an enterprize has prevented its renewal, although there is never a great battle where these Flying Hospitals would not be of the greatest utility and benefit, and save many valuable lives. It is due, however, to Assistant Surgeon General Wood, whose humanity is always paramount to official etiquette, to mention the fact of his hearty approval, and that it was at his request that one of these hospitals was sent to the Army of the Frontier, then at Fayetteville, Arkansas.

During the present year three additional military hospitals were added to those already established in St. Louis, the Marine, the Jefferson Barracks, and the Lawson Hospitals. The necessity for this arose from the large number of sick brought by the hospital steamers from the armies of the Frontier, the South-west, the Tennessee and the Mississippi.

The Marine Hospital was a government institution, originally intended for persons engaged in the navigation of the Mississippi river. It is a four story stone and brick edifice, surrounded by extensive and well shaded grounds, a garden in which the convalescent patients perform a part of the labor, and has every convenience of a model hospitals.

It was opened as a military hospital May the 4th, 1862, and then had accommodations for 150 patients. From that date till May 1st, 1864, it had received 1574 patients, and its per centage of death was 9. During the summer of 1863 its accommodations were enlarged for 100 more patients by the addition of wooden barracks, in which a new and excellent mode of ventilation was introduced by Mr. Leeds of Philadelphia, by means of stoves, drawing fresh air through an air chamber, under the floor, and passing it through the heating chamber of the stoves into the wards. There being also a ridge ventilation at the top of the barracks, and a ventilating shaft in each ward, with openings at the top and bottom of the rooms, no more perfect system of ventilation could possibly be devised, securing at the same time whatever temperature may be desired.

The officers are Assistant Surgeon James H. Peabody, U. S. V., in charge, L. H. Calloway, M. D., Acting Assistant Surgeon, and Rev. James A. Page, Chaplain.

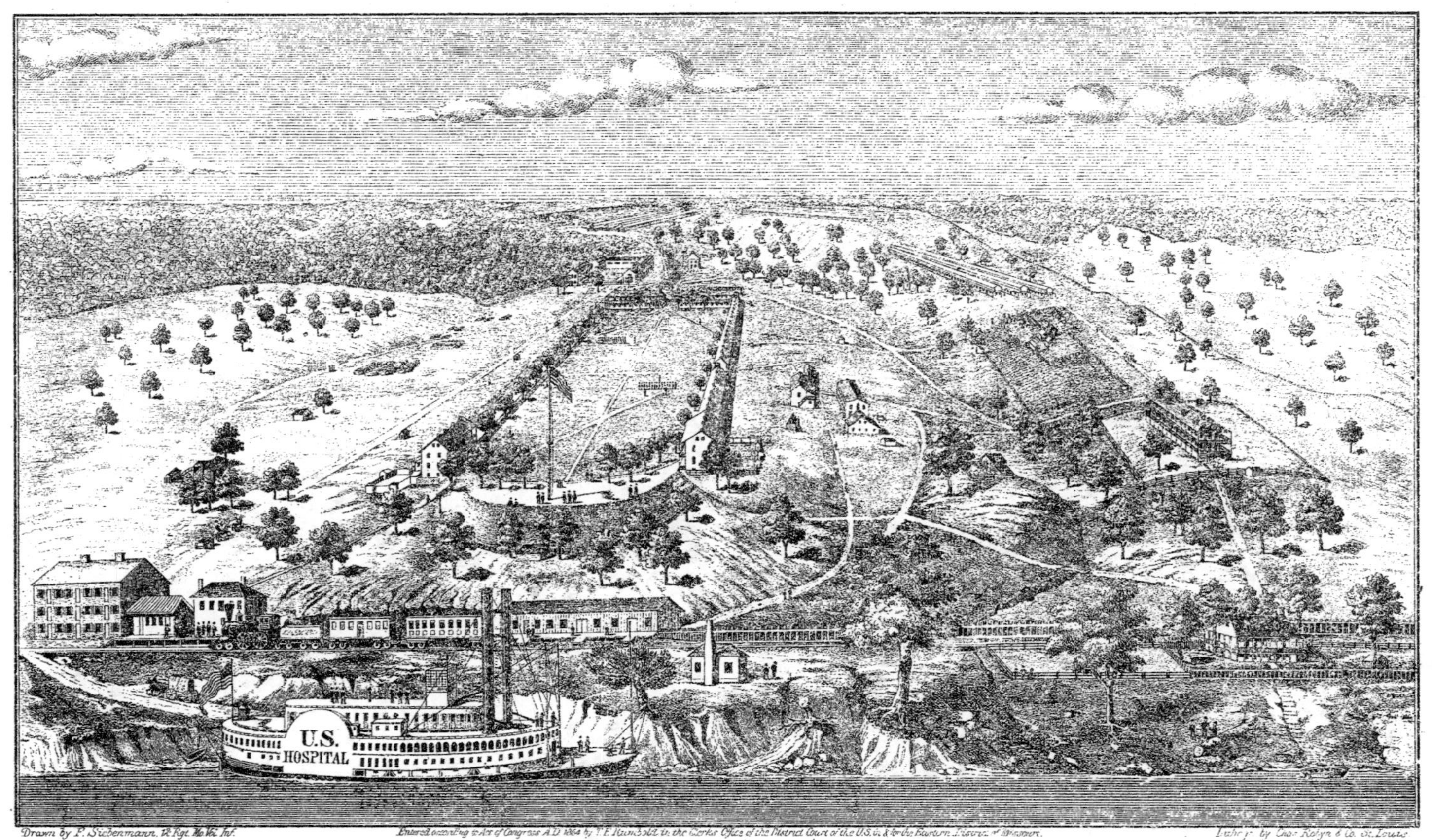

Drawn by F. Siebenmann, 12 Rgt. Mo. Vol. Inf. Entered according to Act of Congress A.D. 1864 by T. F. Rambold in the Clerks Office of the District Court of the U.S. in & for the Eastern District of Missouri. Lith. by Chas. Robyn & Co. St. Louis.

U. S. GENERAL HOSPITAL JEFFERSON BARRACKS. JNO. F. RANDOLPH Surg. U.S.A. in Charge.

Jefferson Barracks was formerly a military post at which United States troops were stationed, situated about twelve miles below St. Louis, on the west bank of the Mississippi river. It consists of long rows of buildings, one and two stories high, with basement kitchens and dining-rooms, and wide piazzas, extending on three sides of a large plat of ground, in the form of a parallelogram, shaded with fine trees, the open end of the grounds being towards the river, with a high flag-staff on the bluff, from which the flag of the Union is always unfurled to the breeze. The old post hospital stands near on an adjoining eminence, and is two stories high, and the post chapel is situated several hundred yards back from the river, in a pleasantly shaded spot, retired from the barracks.

In April, 1862, these buildings, except the post chapel, which is still reserved for worship, were converted into a large hospital, for which purpose they were admirably suited, the rooms being large, having numerous windows on both sides, opposite each other, and the piazzas and shaded walks, affording excellent opportunities for exercise.

Beside the old buildings, the Government, during the summer of 1862, erected others on the ample grounds belonging to it, on the west side, so as to afford accommodations for two thousand five hundred patients. These new buildings are one story high, in triple rows six hundred feet long, divided into wards of three hundred feet each. There are three groups or sets of these new hospitals, some distance apart, the entire grounds in every direction being beautifully shaded by large oak trees. They are so arranged that each group has the central row appropriated to a dining-room, and surgeons', nurses' and stewards' quarters, the outside rows being for sick wards. Besides these improvements, a system of water works has been introduced, with reservoir and pipes, by which the water of the Mississippi is carried through all the buildings.

The institution is in charge of Surgeon J. F. Randolph, U. S. A., assisted by Dr. H. R. Tilton, U. S. A., and P. C. McLane, M. D.; A.

L. Allen, M. D.; T. F. Rumbold, M. D.; Hiram Latham, M. D.; S. Leslie, M. D., and J. J. Marston, M. D. The Post Chaplain, Rev. J. F. Fish, has been stationed here many years, and continues his services, in connection with Rev. S. Pettigrew, Hospital Chaplain.

The number of patients received and treated in this hospital in two years, ending April 30, 1864, is 11,434. The per centage of deaths the first year was eleven and a half, which was much increased by the large number brought to it in a dying condition. The per centage of deaths for the year just ended is nine and eight-tenths.

The Lawson Hospital is situated on the corner of Broadway and Carr streets, and was fitted up during the latter part of the fall of 1862. The edifice was originally intended for a hotel, is seven stories high, and is divided into eight wards, besides office rooms, nurses' quarters, linen room, kitchen, dining hall, and store rooms. It is well ventilated; an average number of seven hundred and fifty cubic feet is allowed to each bed ; and it is provided with a steam engine and elevator, furnished by the Western Sanitary Commission, at an expense of two thousand five hundred dollars. The institution is in charge of Surgeon C. T. Alexander, U. S. A., assisted by W. H. Bradley, M. D.; L. H. Bottomley, M. D., and Wm. Fritz, M. D. Rev. Phillip McKim is Hospital Chaplain.

The hospital was opened January 17th, 1863, since which the whole number of patients received has been 3,021. For the first four months the per centage of deaths was very large, being twenty-five and nine-tenths, which was owing to the fact that during that period it received the wounded from the battles of Vicksburg and Arkansas Post, and the sick from Milliken's Bend and Helena, which were of the worst description, having many hopeless cases both of wounds and of chronic diarrhea, some of whom died as they were being brought into the hospital. The per centage of deaths for the last year, ending April 30th, 1864, has been much less, being 7 8-10.

The diminished per centage of deaths in the military hospitals during the third year of the war, which the statistics of other hospitals will show, is evidence of a most gratifying improvement in the management of these institutions, and in the care and treatment of the sick and wounded soldier. This result has been influenced also by the sifting out from our armies, by death and discharges from the service, during the first two years of the war, all those who were not able to endure its hardships and exposures, those who remain being mainly veteran troops. No war has ever been conducted in which the per cent of deaths from disease has been so small, and the health and vigor of the troops so well maintained; nor one in which there has been so strong a current of sympathy and aid from the people at home towards the soldiers in the field, as in this war for the unity and national supremacy of the American Republic. Civilians, unable to bear arms, men of science and of letters, the orators and poets, and clergy of the land, and the noble and self-sacrificing women of our free commonwealths, have all vied with each other in their efforts to give help and sympathy to the soldier, and to inspire an interest in his welfare. With such an influence to encourage and cheer the armies of the Union, there is an explanation of the health, the spirit, and the unconquerable bravery of our troops, who, under their present tried and able commanders, are bearing the flag of freedom on to victory. May the spirit of liberty continue thus to animate all hearts, and welcome home our brave defenders when the last battle shall be fought, and our peace and prosperity be established on sure foundations.

CHAPTER VII.

General Sherman's First Attack on Vicksburg—Works Assaulted—Severe Losses to the Union Arms—Hospital Steamers bring the Wounded to Memphis and St. Louis—Battle of Arkansas Post—More Wounded brought to St. Louis—Delegation of the Ladies' Union Aid Society of St. Louis—Iowa State Agent—Renewal of the Expedition against Vicksburg by General Grant—Increased Hospital Accommodations required—Visit of Mr. Yeatman to Gen. Grant's Army—His Letter—Benton Barracks Hospital, St. Louis—Additional Hospitals at Memphis—The Floating Hospital, "City of Alton," the "Ruth," and "Glasgow"—Second Visit of Mr. Yeatman to General Grant's Army—His Report—Sanitary Stores sent to Gen. Grant's Army—Fall of Vicksburg—Its Untitled Heroes.

In the latter part of December, 1862, Maj. Gen. W. T. Sherman embarked an army of twenty thousand troops on transports, at Memphis and Helena, and commenced an expedition against Vicksburg, under the direction of Maj. Gen. Grant, who was to co-operate by land, in a movement through Holly Springs to Jackson, taking Vicksburg in the rear. On the 26th of December, the main forces, under Gen. Sherman, disembarked successfully at Johnston's Landing, near the mouth of the Yazoo river, and prepared for an assault the next day on the northern works that defended the city. On the 27th, 28th, and 29th, several attempts were made to take the fortifications, but a stern and terrible resistance was made by the rebels, who outnumbered our forces, and who had the advantage of the strongest natural defenses and artificial earthworks known in modern warfare.

The result of the three days' fighting was a terrible loss in killed and wounded to the Union forces, and a temporary relinquishment of the undertaking. An unforeseen contingency, the capture of Holly Springs, in General Grant's rear, cutting off his communication and his supplies, had compelled his return to that point, and the abandonment of his part of the undertaking, which had enabled the rebels to concentrate their forces at Vicksburg, and accomplish Gen. Sherman's defeat. The wounded of his army were immediately forwarded to the Memphis and St. Louis hospitals by transports and hospital steamers. On their way they were met by a delegation of the Ladies' Union Aid Society, of St. Louis, hastening on the first boats with boxes of sanitary goods, to minister to their necessities.

The Western Commission put in charge of these ladies a large supply of stores, to be used by them or turned over to the surgeons, as they should be needed. The agent of the Commission, Mr. Plattenburg, also went down with Gen. Sherman's expedition from Helena, and was on hand with his sanitary stores immediately after the fighting.

The delegation of the St. Louis Ladies' Union Aid Society consisted of Mrs. Alfred Clapp, the President of the Society, Mrs. J. E. D. Couzins, Mrs. Washington King, Mrs. J. Crawshaw, Mrs. Wm. Clark, and Miss Breckinridge. Besides these there was also a delegation from the Chicago Branch of the U. S. Commission of Mrs. M. A. Livermore and Mrs. Hoge of Chicago, and Mrs. Henrietta J. Colt of Milwaukie; and there was likewise Mrs. Annie Wittenmier, the State agent of the Iowa Sanitary Commission, who had in charge a large supply of sanitary goods from that State. All these noble women were indefatigable in their efforts to relieve and comfort the sick and wounded, and to minister to them.

The disastrous attack on Vicksburg, which ended the year '62, was followed up, almost immediately by another expedition, with the same army, under Gen. J. A. McClernand, assisted by the navy, against Arkansas Post, on the Arkansas river, which was taken, after another severe battle on the 11th of January, '63, with eight thousand prisoners, and a large number of cannon, ordnance stores and small arms, the gunboats "Louisville," "DeKalb," "Cincinnati," and "Lexington," under Admiral Porter, co-operating with the land forces.

The fortifications at Arkansas Post were destroyed, and the expedition then returned up the river to Helena and Memphis, bringing along several hundred wounded on transports, who suffered many privations, the surgeons being poorly provided with the means of making them comfortable. The boats were much crowded, the weather was cold, draughts of air were blowing through the cabins, the sick and wounded men had to lie on the floors, and there were not nurses enough to take care of them.

On reaching Helena a portion of the St. Louis delegation of the Ladies' Union Aid Society, who had just returned from Vicksburg, went on board these transports, took such sanitary stores with them as were needed, and remained on them till they reached St. Louis, bestowing the tenderest care and nursing upon those poor suffering and wounded men.

The severity of these wounds, the unavoidable exposure in winter, the long passage to St. Louis, both of those from Vicksburg, as well as of those from Arkansas Post, resulted in the loss of many of these brave men, and a great percentage of deaths followed in the Lawson Hospital at St. Louis, where most of them were taken, as well as of the very sick, from Helena, being 25 9-10th per cent of all who were admitted during that winter, till the first of the next June.

It was at this time, while there were so many sick in the camps and hospitals of the army in Tennessee and Arkansas, during the worst winter known for many years, and when so many wounded were thrown upon our care, that additional hospitals were opened at St. Louis and Memphis, and additional hospital steamers fitted up to ply to and fro on the Mississippi river, between the army and the well-furnished and well-managed hospitals farther north.

This was done also in view of the renewal of operations against Vicksburg. On the failure of Gen. Grant's movement through Mississippi, to take Jackson, and attack Vicksburg in the rear, while Gen. Sherman attacked the city on the north side, he returned to, Holly Springs, punished the recreant commander, Col. R. C. Murphy who had surrendered that post without any proper effort to defend it, by dismissal from the service, and thence proceeded with his army to Memphis, where he embarked his forces on transports for Young's Point and Milliken's Bend, La. Here he landed his troops on the 29th of January. It does not come within the legitimate object of this work to give even a sketch of military operations, beyond what is necessary to show how the Sanitary Commission followed the army and navy, and improved its opportunities of usefulness.

During February and March, while the army of Gen. Grant was occupying the low region of country above Vicksburg, on the Louisiana shore, trying to change the bed of the river, by cutting a canal across the large bend, opposite the city; while gunboats and transports, with troops, were sent to explore the bayous leading to the Yazoo and Red rivers; and while an expedition was sent to open the Yazoo Pass, to effect a passage through the Cold Water and Tallahatchie rivers to the Yazoo, by which to destroy rebel vessels in that river, capture Yazoo City, and take Vicksburg in the rear, the Mississippi was overflowing the low lands in every direction, the camping grounds of many of the regiments were flooded, the rains were incessant, and, as a necessary consequence, there was a large amount of sickness in the army. Exaggerated reports were circulated by letter writers through the Northern press, and much anxiety and uneasiness were felt in regard to the health of the troops.

At this time Mr. Yeatman, the President of the Western Commission, went down to make a personal inspection, and on his return, on the 13th of March, published a letter, giving an account of his visit, and of the actual state of things. In this letter he says:

"For a short time after the landing of the army at and near Young's Point, consequent upon long confinement upon transports, there was much sickness; but the health of the troops improved rapidly, and the per centage of sickness is below what I have generally found it in camps in other portions of the country which I have visited. Besides many others, I visited every regiment in Sherman's corps, which was reported in the worst condition. While in some of the new regiments the amount of sickness was large, in others it was unusually small. The great danger to be apprehended was from want of vegetable diet, symptoms of scurvy having already made their appearance."

Mr. Yeatman recommended that the friends of the soldiers should send large quantities of vegetables, fruits, and pickles, and the Commission at once sent a large supply, and directed its agent, Mr. Plattenburg, to proceed immediately and establish his headquarters with the army near Vicksburg.

Mr. Yeatman remarked, with great satisfaction, the interest taken by Generals Sherman and Grant in the health of their troops. He says of the former: "I saw Gen. Sherman going through the camps on foot, giving particular directions in regard to sanitary regulations. No one could look after his men more carefully than he does. While he maintains a strict discipline, he mingles with and goes among his men to ascertain personally their wants. He has a kind word for all, and is greeted, by his men, as one who cares for, and thinks of their comfort. With the sick he is as delicate and tender as a woman. I am thus particular in mentioning General Sherman's corps, as my attention was particularly directed to it, owing to reports which had been made to me."

After describing the ample arrangements made for the care of the sick and wounded, he remarked still further: "Gen. Grant is determined to have provision made for the sick equal to any contingency that may arise, and before long will quarter his army on high ground, on the opposite side of the river. Assistant Surgeon General Wood is accomplishing, and will accomplish, all that is possible to be done."

While these arrangements were being carried out near the scene of conflict, the Assistant Surgeon General was making extensive preparations, at St. Louis and Memphis, to be well provided against future emergencies. Under his directions, the large amphitheatre building in the old fair grounds at Benton Barracks, a few miles northwest from St. Louis, and north of the St. Charles road, was taken possession of by the Government for hospital purposes. It was enclosed, provided with windows, floored, partitioned, divided into wards, thoroughly whitewashed, furnished with iron bedsteads and good beds, and converted into one of the largest, most thoroughly ventilated and best hospitals in the United States, capable of accommodating two thousand five hundred patients. Numerous other buildings, near the main edifice, on the same grounds, formerly used by the Agricultural Society for its exhibitions, were used for officers' quarters, medical dispensary, commissary rooms, special diet kitchens, &c., and the fine walks and splendid shade added much to the beauty and attractiveness of the place.

The institution was at first placed in charge of Surgeon Ira Russell, U. S. V., under whose administration it was conducted with entire success. It was opened March 1st, 1863, and during the following three months received two thousand and forty-two patients. For that period the per centage of deaths was only four and a half of the whole number. From June 1st, 1863, to May 1st, 1864, there were four thousand eight hundred and ninety-eight patients received, and the per centage of deaths was seven and one-tenth.

In this hospital there was appointed an excellent corps of female nurses, who were placed under the immediate oversight and direction of a supervisor of nurses, acting under the surgeon in charge, which position was ably and successfully filled by Miss Emily Parsons, of Cambridge, Mass. The good order, attention to duty, and faithfulness of the nurses, in the several wards, were greatly promoted by this system. Fortunately for the experiment it had the hearty approval of the surgeon in charge ; and it is due to him, as well as the supervisor of nurses, to say that probably, in no hospital in the United States, was the nursing of the sick and wounded brought to greater perfection than here.

Auxiliary to this system the Ladies' Union Aid Society also established a special diet kitchen, in one of the buildings in the amphitheatre, which is wholly conducted by members of that society, provided with delicacies for the sick, wines, stimulants, &c., to which the Western Sanitary Commission also contributes, and from this kitchen any delicate food needed for the very sick can always be ordered, by the surgeons, and be immediately prepared.

For a few months of the autumn of '63, Surgeon Russell was relieved by Surgeon J. H. Grove, U. S. V., who conducted the institution on the same principles, and under whom it maintained the same high character.

In the winter of 1863–4 Benton Barracks became a recruiting station for colored troops ; hospital accommodations were needed for the sick of the colored regiments ; several of the wards were appropriated for their use ; and Dr. Grove, having been assigned to another position of responsibility and trust, Dr. Russell was again placed in charge. Under his management the institution still maintains its original character ; the female nurses act under Miss Parsons, as supervisor ; the special diet kitchen is still maintained, in charge of Mrs. Shepard Wells, of the Ladies' Union Aid Society ; and the sick soldiers, whether of the white troops or of the regiments of African descent, each occupying separate wards, are treated with the care and kind attention due to the soldiers of the Union.

Besides the general hospital, there is also a post hospital at Benton Barracks, likewise in charge of Surgeon Russell. During the fall of 1863, and winter of '64, many of the sick of the new colored regiments were treated here. The whole number of patients received was 6140, and the per centage of deaths 8 2-10. Female nurses are provided for this hospital by the Western Sanitary Commission, the Government only allowing them to the general hospitals.

At Memphis, by direction of Assistant Surgeon General Wood, several additional hospitals were fitted up there in the winter and spring of 1863. They were generally the largest and best buildings in the city, having been originally designed for hotels, or blocks of stores, four and five stories high. These hospitals were named the Overton, Washington, Gayoso, Jackson, Jefferson, Marine, Webster, Union, Gangrene, and Officers', and were capable of accommodating about 5000 sick and wounded men. During the summer of '63, while Gen. Grant's army was operating against Vicksburg, and after the fall of that city, these hospitals were filled, and there was a constant demand for sanitary stores. Maj. T. P. Robb, of Illinois, acted as a Sanitary agent for that State, and also for the Western Sanitary Commission, and distributed largely both to the regiments encamped at Memphis, and to the hospitals.

Many commissioned officers having been wounded at the battles of Vicksburg, were also without their pay, and were not allowed by regulations the ordinary accommodations of enlisted men. Their condition being made known to the Commission, it furnished a complete outfit of every thing necessary for a hospital of one hundred beds, called the Officers' hospital.

The United States Sanitary Commission also maintained a well-supplied agency at Memphis, in charge of Dr. H. A. Warriner, an able and efficient officer, who had a general supervision of the work of that Commission, on the Mississippi river, and often acted in friendly co-operation with the agents of the Western Commission.

During the same winter and spring the large and splendid steamer "*City of Alton*," was used as a floating hospital, being fitted up for this purpose; and the steamer "*Ruth*," of equal dimensions and magnificence, (since destroyed), the steamer "*Glasgow*," and a number of smaller boats were likewise used as transports for conveying the sick and wounded from the Lower Mississippi to the hospitals at Memphis and St. Louis. Besides these, the large and commodious floating hospital "*Nashville*," was fitted up so as to accommodate one thousand patients, and located permanently near Milliken's Bend, in charge of

Surgeon L. D. Strawbridge, U. S. A.; and the hospital steamers "*City of Memphis*," and "*D. A. January*," capable of accommodating twelve hundred more, were under the order of the Medical Director, either for transportation to hospitals, or for the care of the sick and wounded for any length of time that might be needed there. The Medical Purveyor also had a boat set apart exclusively for medical supplies of all kinds, with cots and bedding sufficient to extemporize several other floating hospitals, in case of necessity. Two large boats were likewise turned over to the United States and Western Sanitary Commissions, whose agents were constantly receiving and distributing supplies. No army was ever better provided for than the army of Gan. Grant at this period, and to these efforts to keep up the health and vigor of the troops was due much of that courage and endurance which resulted in the splendid victories that crowned our arms, in the series of great battles fought at Fort Gibson, Raymond, Jackson, Champion Hills, the Big Black river, and before the entrenchments of Vicksburg, to the fall of that city.

When at last this Gibraltar of the enemy fell into our possession, with thirty thousand prisoners of war, there were many sick and wounded men in the camps and hospitals around the city. These had still to be cared for and brought up the river, away from the heats of summer in that Southern latitude.

At the time of Gen. Grant's investment of Vicksburg, and the two unsuccessful assaults made on the rebel works on the 19th and the 22d of May, there were four thousand five hundred of our brave troops wounded. The President of the Western Sanitary Commission made a second visit at that time in charge of the steamer "*Champion*," loaded with commissary and sanitary stores. A large portion of the sanitary goods, and many tons of ice, having been furnished by the merchants of St. Louis, Mr. Yeatman, on his return, publishhd a report of his visit, in which he says:

"On the evening of the 26th of May I left here on the steamer

"*Champion*," accompanied by a corps of surgeons, nurses and dressers of wounds, numbering fifty-five in all, *with some two hundred and fifty tuns of sanitary supplies*, besides cots, mattrasses, and every thing necessary for taking care of a thousand wounded men, in case of necessity, the latter articles having been furnished by order of the Assistant Surgeon General R. C. Wood.

"We did not arrive at Chickasaw Bluffs, near Vicksburg, until the evening of the 31st of May, where we found that the number of the wounded had been greatly exaggerated, the actual number not exceeding four thousand five hundred. The arrangements of the Medical Department were most excellent, and the transportation of the sick and wounded, on the hospital steamer, "*D. A. January*," in charge of Surgeon A. H. Huff, were most perfect. I found that the greater part of the wounded, who required attention, and who could be removed, had been attended to. Of those who had been thus cared for there were about 1,900; and about 2,000 more, who were but slightly wounded, were treated in division hospitals, together with a few hundred who were too severely wounded to be moved. The division hospitals were being consolidated with the army corps hospitals, which were to be placed in shady, sequestered spots, where an abundance of pure, fresh water could be had.

"The wounded being so well provided for it was not necessary that our steamer should be used for hospital purposes; the hospital beds, bedding, and supplies were turned over to the proper medical officers, and the dressers of wounds and nurses were placed where they could be most useful, some of them in hospitals and others on hospital steamers. By the time we arrived at Vicksburg all sanitary stores had become completely exhausted, and the new supplies, in my charge, were greatly needed. They were at once placed in the hands of our Agent, Mr. A. W. Plattenburg, by whom they were distributed, most liberally, whenever they were most wanted. Blessings were invoked, by both Surgeons and men, for this timely care in providing for them, in the great extremity which always succeeds a series of battles, and which can only be fully provided for in this way. No parched and thirsty soil ever drank the dews of heaven, with more avidity, than did those wounded men receive the beneficent gifts and comforts, sent to them through this Commission."

The number of articles sent to Gen. Grant's army from the Western Commission during the month of June, preceding the fall of Vicksburg, was 114,697, consisting of 3,090 hospital shirts, 3,080 hospital drawers, 1,260 sheets, 4,400 bandages, 2,412 bottles of Catawba wine, 1,337 cans of fresh fruit, 1,976 cans of condensed milk, 10,000 lemons, 1,600 gallons of lager beer, 5,477 lbs. dried apples, 2,400 lbs. dried peaches, 2,088 lbs. codfish, 1,850 lbs. herring, 11,710 lbs. crackers, 23,060 lbs. ice, 1,800 chickens, 3,171 dozen eggs, 3,068 lbs. butter, 1,840 lbs. corn meal, 3,145 bushels potatoes, 2,500 fans, 6,004 books and pamphlets, and of the following articles in similar proportions: Blankets, pillows, socks, slippers, handkerchiefs, towels, lbs. of rags, lbs. of lint, eye shades, oil silk pads, pin cushions, rolls of adhesive plaster, tourniquets, crutches, back rests, close stools, spit cups, sponges, splints, air beds, bottles of whisky, bottles of brandy, bottles of Catawba bitters, bottles of ginger wine, bottles of cassia syrup, bottles of blackberry syrup, lbs. of farina, lbs. of corn starch, lbs. of oat meal, lbs. of arrowroot, lbs. of tapioca, lbs. of sago, lbs. of pinola, lbs. of flaxseed, lbs. of cassia, lbs. of allspice, lbs. of mustard, lbs. of nutmegs, lbs. of pepper, bottles of pepper sauce, bottles of horseradish, bottles of tomato catsup, bottles of cranberry sauce, bottles of flavoring extracts, cans of clams and oysters, cans of spiced tripe, cans of jelly, cans of condensed soup, cans of cocoa paste, lbs. of chocolate, cans of portable lemonade, gallons of ale, bottles of drugs, bottles of extract of ginger, lbs. of dried small fruit, lbs. of dried beef, lbs. of extract of beef, lbs. of mackerel, lbs. of cheese, lbs. of bread, lbs. of zwieback, lbs. of coffee, lbs, of tea, lbs. of sugar, lbs.

of sour krout, gallons of pickles, gallons of vinegar, bottles of fine pickles, lbs. of carbonate of soda, lbs. of saleratus, lbs. of citric acid, lbs. of castile soap, Cook's Manual, stationery, faucets, combs and brushes, lbs. of hops, lbs. of tobacco, bread trays, water coolers, scales, cooking stoves, brooms, tin cups, tin basins, tin plates, tin boilers, tin buckets, tin dippers, tin skimmers, coffee pots, tea pots, spoons, stew pans, cork screws, knives and forks, and iron boilers.

Fortunate was it for these brave men that so much preparation and provision had been made for their comfort, and that loving hearts and kind hands had labored for them at home, sending contributions and agents, and volunteer surgeons and nurses, after them, wherever the fortunes of war had led them, to assist in binding up their wounds, in nursing them when sick, and in making them whole. On the fall of Vicksburg, on the following 4th of July, none rejoiced more than these untitled heroes, in the celebration of that day, by so great a victory, and none were more worthy to claim their share of its honors, and to partake in the glory of this, the greatest achievement of the war.

CHAPTER VIII.

Soldiers' Homes at Columbus, Ky., Memphis, Vicksburg, and Helena—Over 150,000 Soldier Guests Entertained—Further Account of the St. Louis Hospitals—Whole Number of Patients Treated—Number of Deaths—Per centage of Deaths—The Military Prisons at St. Louis and Alton, Ill.—Humane Treatment of Sick Prisoners.

On Mr. Yeatman's first visit to the army of Gen. Grant, in the winter of '63, he became satisfied of the necessity of Soldiers' Homes at Memphis, Tenn., and Columbus, Ky., where there were many troops stationed, and many others constantly arriving, either going home discharged, or on furlough to visit their friends, or returning to their regiments, being frequently without means to pay hotel expenses, and needing a place of refreshment and rest. The change of transportation from the river to the railroads, leading to Jackson and Corinth, made this the more necessary.

On the 13th of February, '63, the Soldiers' Home at Memphis was opened for the reception of guests. According to previous arrangement made by the President of the Western Sanitary Commission with Gen. T. C. Hamilton, then in command of the 16th army corps, the large residence on Beal street, known as the "Hunt Mansion," was turned over to Mr. O. E. Waters, as agent of the Commission, for this purpose.

It had formerly been the head-quarters of Maj. Gen. Grant, and more recently of Gen. Hamilton, and was the property of a Mr. Wm. Richardson Hunt, a very wealthy planter, owning a great number of slaves, and now a colonel in the rebel army, many of his slaves still residing in Memphis and providing for themselves. He spent over forty thousand dollars in building and beautifying this mansion with its elegant grounds, little dreaming that in doing this he was preparing so comfortable a home for the soldiers of the Union, and the defenders of the flag he himself dishonored by his infidelity and treason. When the city of Memphis was captured by the United States navy he was among the first to flee, with his fellow traitors, and abandon his home and country for an uncertain abode at Atlanta, Georgia.

When the Home was made ready for guests a card was published inviting the weary soldier to come and partake of its hospitalities, and it was not long till the place was much sought for, and groups of soldiers, dusty and travel-worn, could be seen occupying its piazzas and pleasant rooms, or sitting beneath its evergreen arbors and magnolia shades.

The Superintendent, in his annual report, gives the following account of the opening of the institution:

"Our first guests were brought in by Mrs. Governor Harvey. She found them wandering through the streets, sadly in need of a kind friend to give them assistance and care. One of them, a little drummer boy of the 29th Wisconsin Infantry, when brought in and laid upon a soft mattress, exclaimed, with tears in his eyes, 'Oh, how pleasant this is!' Brave little drummer boy! his spirit found a brighter home and a softer couch ere the morrow's sun arose.

"During the first three months we were confined exclusively to the care of discharged and invalid soldiers, very often having from twenty to thirty helpless men at a time, when papers must be examined, pay collected and comfortable transportation secured, on some steamer going North. Many of these men I found lying upon the hard pavements in the streets, and on the bluff, near the steamboat landing, in a helpless condition, with no friend to assist them. Three-fourths of them were delayed here, from one to eight weeks, on account of imperfect papers. If the officers in our army, having this duty to perform, only knew of the suffering and anguish caused by their carelessness, they would certainly look well to the careful and correct execution of the soldier's discharge papers and final statements. Many a weak, war-worn soldier, with his steps turned toward his Northern home, full of bright anticipations and cheering hopes that he will soon be mingling with the loved ones there, when told that his papers are defective, and rejected by the paymaster, and that they will have to be returned to his regiment for correction, has felt his heart sink within him, and the radiant smile has passed away from his face, in the bitterness of his disappointment. In some instances, before their papers have returned, they have waited, unable to go home, sinking in health, until their final discharge came from the court of Heaven, and, without seeing their loved ones on earth again, they went up to their heavenly home, and their eternal reward.

"Since the Home was established, thirteen deaths have occurred within its walls. This number is small, comparatively, with the number of very sick men we have entertained.

"After the first of May, '63, soldiers of all classes were admitted to the Home, and our numbers began to increase rapidly. The least number entertained in a single day was six, and the greatest number three hundred and fifty. After the siege of Vicksburg was over, and our army sent to other scenes of action, the number of *sick* materially decreased, and our attention was directed more to the care of well men, providing food, transportation, etc."

Of this class of guests the number has steadily increased, and the usefulness of the Home was never greater than at the present time. From its establishment, February 18th, 1863, to May 1st, 1864, the whole number of guests entertained has been 25,830, the number of meals furnished 55,894, and the number of lodgings provided 18,986. Of these guests the record shows them to have been largely Illinois, Missouri, Iowa, Wisconsin, and Indiana troops, with considerable numbers from Ohio, Michigan, Minnesota, and other States. The soldiers from Illinois stopping at this Home, to the 1st of March, were 3018;

from Missouri, 1,524; from Iowa, 1,289; the remainder from other States.

Besides the regular guests entertained here, often the wife, mother, sister, or father of the sick soldier, accompanying him home, and having limited resources, have been received as guests, and members of the United States Christian Commission, engaged in the work of ministering to the army, have also been welcomed to its hospitality, and their religious services in the house have given it a religious and moral character that was highly beneficial to its inmates.

From the opening of this Home, to the present date, it has been under the superintendence of Mr. O. E. Waters, whose services have been constant, faithful, and satisfactory, in the highest degree. For several months he was assisted by Miss A. L. Ostram, as matron, who resigned her position to fill a similar one at Cairo, Illinois. She was succeeded by Mrs. Lucy E. Starr, who has occupied the position for nearly a year, and has imparted so cheerful a spirit to the Home, and been so unremitting in her labors that her praise is every where spoken by those who have been the guests of the institution.

On the 16th of February, '63, the Soldiers' Home at Columbus, Ky., was opened, and has entertained many thousand soldier guests. It was at first superintended by Mr. Brown, and for a short time by Mr. Geo. E. Wyeth, when Chaplain Ephraim Nute, became superintendent in the spring of '63, and continued in charge till September of the same year, when he went to New Orleans to establish another Home for the Commission in that city.* He was succeeded at Columbus by Mr. S. J. Orange, the present excellent and faithful superintendent. The first matron was Mrs. S. A. Plummer, who was assisted by Miss Ida

*The Soldiers' Home at New Orleans was duly established in October, 1862, by Mr. Nute, acting as the agent of the Western Sanitary Commission, under a special order from Maj. Gen. Grant. He was provided with furniture, stores, and funds for this purpose, to the value of several thousand dollars, and the Home, on its first opening, was crowded with guests. Late in November it was transferred to the U. S. Commission, under whose auspices it is still continued. Rev. Mr. Nute, from the date of this transfer, ceased to be the agent of the Western Commission, and soon after returned to his regiment.

Johnson, and to both these ladies great praise is due, for their devotion to the interests of the Home, and their kind and faithful service to the soldiers, who were their guests. In August, '63, Mrs. Plummer was transferred to the Soldiers' Home, at Vicksburg, where she has continued as matron to the present date. She was succeeded at Columbus by Mrs. Orange, who has performed the duties of matron with the utmost satisfaction. Many letters have been received from soldiers who have been the guests of this home, testifying their appreciation of the services of Mr. and Mrs. Orange, and their gratitude for the kind hospitalities received.

The whole number of guests entertained at the Columbus Home from February 16th, 1863, to May 1st, 1864, has been 52,259, the number of meals furnished, 96,694, and the number of lodgings provided, 20,315. The number of troops from Illinois, among the above guests, for the year ending February 16th, 1864, was 2,243; from Iowa, 888; from Wisconsin, 1,211; from Missouri, 864; the remainder being from the other Western States.

The Soldiers' Home, at Vicksburg, was opened August 6th 1863, with Mr. R. K. Foster for Superintendent, and Mrs. S. A. Plummer for Matron. On the taking of this city, it became the base of movements into the interior, and with its garrison and the moving of troops, and the changing of transportation from the river to the land it was foreseen that a Soldiers' Home would be necessary here. A large and good building was obtained from the Government for the purpose, furniture and supplies were sent forward from St. Louis, sufficient for two hundred guests, and from the opening of the institution to the present date, it has been crowded to its utmost capacity.

Mr. Foster continued in charge till the 28th of November, when he was succeeded by Mr. N. M. Mann, the present competent and excellent superintendent. Mr. Foster continued to act as Sanitary agent for the Commission, at Vicksburg, from the transfer of Mr.

Plattenburg to the 15th army corps, till in January, 1864, when he was transferred to Helena, Ark., to open a Home at that place.

Mrs. Plummer has continued to act as matron of the Vicksburg Home from the beginning, and devoted herself to its duties with her usual zeal and interest in the welfare of the soldiers. She has been ably assisted in her labors by Miss Hattie Wiswall, assistant matron, another of the excellent and devoted women, who have been untiring in their services to our brave defenders in arms, from the beginning of the war. For many months this Home has also enjoyed the voluntary labors of Mrs. Governor Harvey, of Wisconsin, who, finding it crowded with guests, has lent a helping hand in its management, besides giving much of her time and energy to the interests of the poor freedmen and their families, and to the destitute Union refugees. Mr. Mann has also labored most efficiently for these people, of which an account will be given in a chapter devoted to that subject.

The number of soldiers entertained at the Vicksburg Home, from August 6th, 1863, to May 1st, 1864, has been 49,738; the number of meals furnished 81,144, and the number of lodgings provided 30,882. Of the guests for six months, 3,866 have been from Illinois regiments; 1,919 from Iowa regiments; 829 from Wisconsin regiments; 451 from Missouri regiments; the rest being from other States.

There have also been entertained at this Home quite a number of persons, laboring as agents and teachers to the freedmen, and members of the Christian Commission, who, being engaged in a similar work of benevolence and Christianity, and the city being without sufficient hotel accommodations, have been welcomed, from time to time, to its hospitalities.

On February 11th, 1864, another Soldiers' Home was opened at Helena, Ark. Having a large army in Arkansas, and many troops passing through Helena, on their way to and from their regiments, it was deemed advisable, with the concurrence of Brig. Gen. N. B. Buford, commanding that post, to establish a Home there. In this work Gen. Buford and his excellent lady afforded much aid, and one of the churches of the place having been assigned for the purpose, with new buildings erected for office room, kitchen, and dining hall, the institution was soon comfortably fitted up with bedsteads, beds, bedding, kitchen furniture, stores, etc., sent from the Western Commission, and was immediately filled with guests. For a brief period Mr. R. K. Foster acted as superintendent, when he returned to St. Louis, and Rev. John I. Herrick, chaplain of the 29th Wisconsin infantry, being on detached service at Helena, was detailed by Gen. Buford, at the request of the Commission, to act as superintendent, and continues in charge at this date. Mrs. H. A. Haines, an experienced and capable person, was sent down to be matron, and has filled the position thus far very successfully, and with entire satisfaction to the Commission. During the three months the Home has been established, it has entertained 3527 guests, furnished 8062 meals, and and provided 3162 lodgings.

Summing up the statistics of all these Homes, including the one at St. Louis, it will be found that there have been entertained in them 152,200 soldier guests, 327,786 meals furnished, and 96,635 lodgings provided, and that of this number there have been 14,703 guests from Illinois regiments, 7,359 from Missouri regiments, and 8,711 from Iowa regiments, up to March 1st, 1864, the remainder being divided among soldiers from Indiana, Ohio, Michigan, Wisconsin, Minnesota, Kansas, Nebraska, Colorado, Pennsylvania, New Jersey, New York, and the U. S. regulars.

Besides the hospitals of St. Louis, of which a previous account has been given, there are two Post hospitals, one on Hickory street, and the other at Benton Barracks, the Gratiot Prison hospital, and the Small-pox hospital on Duncan's Island. The first of these was originally a General hospital, and there was formerly a Post hospital at Schofield Barracks, in the immediate vicinity, on Chouteau Avenue, which was consolidated with it November 1st, 1863. The whole number of patients received at Hickory street, to that date, was 1826, and the per centage of deaths was 6 1-10, and at Schofield Barracks the number of patients received was 206, and the per centage of deaths 4 3-10. At the Military Prison hospital, in McDowell's College, Gratiot street, the number of patients received to May 1st, '64, is 3,514, and the per centage of deaths 11 4-10. The surgeon in charge is B. B. Breed, U. S. V. The number of patients received at the Small-pox hospital to June 1st, '63, was 871, and the per centage of deaths 22 9-10. The number of prisoners received at the same institution, for the same period, was 162, and the per centage of deaths 34 1-2. The great mortality of prisoners in this hospital, and at McDowell's College, Gratiot street, was owing largely to the neglected and exhausted condition in which they fell into our hands. No statistics have been received from this institution, for this work, although requested of the surgeon in charge.

The number of patients treated at the Post hospital on Hickory street, from November 1st, 1863, to May 1st, 1864, is 1,412, and the per centage of deaths 2 9-10. The institution is in charge of Frank W. White, M. D., A. A. Surgeon, U. S. A.

The Good Samaritan, the Fifth street, the Elliott, and the New House of Refuge hospitals, having been discontinued, the statistics of them may be found in the second Annual Report of the Commission, June 1st, 1863.

The whole number of patients treated in the hospitals of St. Louis, including those at Jefferson and Benton Barracks, up to May 1st, '64, is 61,744, the number that have died is 5,684, and the per centage of deaths 9 1-10.

The military prisons of St. Louis have, from the beginning of the war, received the constant attention of the Western Sanitary Commission, and sanitary stores have been issued to them in all cases of urgent need, upon the requisitions of the surgeon in charge.

In November, 1862, the hospital of Gratiot Street Prison, in McDowell's College, used exclusively for prisoners of war, was found to be much crowded, and the building also needed a thorough renovation and cleansing. The facts were reported to Maj. Gen. Curtis, then commanding the department, and the crowded condition both of the prison and the hospital, was obviated by sending a considerable number to the large military prison at Alton, Illinois. The Commission then had the whole interior of the prison and hospital thoroughly cleansed and whitewashed, by wards, and the condition of things was much improved. Assistant Surgeon General Wood also assigned two surgeons to the prison, and made its hospital entirely separate, with its own arrangements complete.

The Commission made an effort at the same time to induce the government to rent other and larger buildings for a military hospital, but the necessity having in a measure ceased, with a removal of a part of the patients to Alton, it was not successful.

The Myrtle Street Prison, in which military offences by United States troops are punished, was also thoroughly inspected at the same time, and measures of improvement were carried into effect.

The Commission has extended its inspections to the military prison at Alton, Illinois, and furnished supplies, to most urgent cases of need, on the requisition of the surgeon in charge. This prison is the same formerly occupied as the Illinois State Penitentiary, which was removed to Joliet, just before the breaking out of the war. It has a large area of ground, 420 by 323 feet, enclosed by a high stone wall, with the prison buildings inside, is in a healthy location, within a few rods of the Mississippi river, on the east side, has good water, excellent drainage, a free circulation of pure air, and could not be better adapted to the purposes for which it is used.

A committee from the Western Sanitary Commission visited it in December, 1862, and in a published report of the visit, said, "We found the hospital to be a good, brick structure, 104 by 35 feet, well ventilated, but insufficiently warmed. It contains sixty-three patients. Many of the sick were needing proper under-clothing. Most of the buildings in the enclosure stand isolated, with considerable ground between them, so that in a moral and sanitary point of view, they are very favorably situated. The prisoners are furnished abundantly with good wholsome food, and they appear to be entirely satisfied with the kind treatment of officers and attendants. The clothes of the prisoners are washed outside the walls, by laundresses, paid out of the prison funds. There is also a washing apparatus on the ground, with a plentiful supply of hot water, and soap, which is freely resorted to by the inmates."

There were then 700 prisoners confined in this prison, with accommodations for 1,300. Since then, it has frequently contained over one thousand. During a recent visit of the Secretary of the Commission, he found the hospital in an excellent condition, in charge of Surgeon T. A. Worrell, U.S.V., Dr. Hez. Williams, A. A. Surgeon, with beds for three hundred patients; the floors clean, and the arrangements similar to the military hospitals for our own troops. There were 120 sick prisoners out of 1000, then in prison. The four female nurses in attendance were Sisters of Charity. A chaplain is also allowed the prison, Rev. Father Vehay, of the Catholic church. A supply of sanitary stores has been recently sent to the Surgeon in charge, on his requisition. The small-pox patients are treated in tents, on the island, just opposite Alton. There were recently but few cases of this disease.

Those who die in this prison, are buried in a ground about two miles out of the city, set apart especially for that purpose. They are furnished with a coffin, the same as the Union soldier, and are in all respects decently interred. Head boards, with the initials of their names are placed at each grave, so that there can be no difficulty identifying the spot.

The statistics of the prison and hospital were recently requested, for the purpose of giving a more complete statement for this work, but were refused by Brig. Gen. Copeland, commanding the post. It is believed that the facts would show that this prison and its hospital have been conducted in a manner creditable to the humanity of the United States Government, and would convey, by contrast, a terrible rebuke to the inhumanity with which our soldiers have been starved and treated in the prisons of the South.

CHAPTER IX.

Sanitary Stores sent to the Army of Gen. Davidson, at Bloomfield, Mo.—Part of them Captured by Guerrillas—Narrow Escape of the Agent—Stores sent to the Army of Gen. Steele, at Duvall's Bluff and Little Rock—Agency Established at Little Rock—Acknowledgments—Stores sent to Fort Blunt, Cherokee Nation—Acknowledgment—Stores sent to Colored troops at Milliken's Bend, Goodrich's Landing, and Vicksburg—Letters of Rev. Dr. Eliot and Mr. Yeatman—Books and Instruction furnished to Colored Troops at Benton Barracks—Letter from Col. A. Watson Webber—Stores sent to Nashville and Murfreesboro, Tenn.—Agency at Huntsville, Ala.—Stores sent to the Naval Flotilla—Veteran Regiments Entertained at St. Louis—Stores to the 33d Illinois Infantry—Acknowledgment—Stores to Banks' Army on Red River—Several Important Questions Answered—Do the Soldiers get any of the Sanitary Stores?—Illustrations—Accountability of Agents—Hospitals, Regiments, Hospital Steamers and Gunboats supplied with Sanitary Stores—List of Female Nurses who have proved their worth in the Hospitals of Saint Louis.

During the month of August, 1863, Brig. Gen. Davidson, commanding a force of cavalry, was stationed at Bloomfield, Mo., preparatory to a movement on Little Rock. His sick were to be left at that place, in hospital, and, in accordance with his request, the Commission sent an agent there, Mr. H. J. Waterman, with a large supply of sanitary stores. On the way from Cape Girardeau to Bloomfield, with a commissary train, in which six of the wagons were loaded with the stores of the Commission, the train was attacked, while encamped at night, by a band of guerrillas of the enemy, twelve soldiers and teamsters were killed, the mules were carried off, and the wagons, commissary stores, and sanitary goods set fire to and burned, with the exception of two wagons, which happened to contain sanitary stores. The guerrillas then made their escape, and Mr. Waterman, with the captain of the train, who had narrowly escaped, proceeded on the next day to Bloomfield, in a very crippled condition. On arriving there, what was left of the sanitary stores were distributed to the sick, in hospital, where they were much needed, and most thankfully received, and Mr. Waterman returned to Cape Girardeau, where he had left about half of his original supply, being unable to procure transportation.

Previous to his reaching Bloomfield, Gen. Davidson had moved on, towards Little Rock, with his available forces, and as it was now known that Maj. Gen. Steele was about to move from Helena, with a large force, to the same point, it was deemed advisable, by the Commission, that a permanent agent should accompany this expedition. Mr. Waterman was accordingly ordered to proceed, from Cape Girardeau, with his stores, to Helena, by the river, and there join the command of Gen. Steele. On his arrival at Helena, the expedition had moved as far as Clarendon, on White river, and the weather being warm, it was reported that already there were many sick at that point. Mr. Waterman, with difficulty, procured transportation, and reached Clarendon, where, being himself taken very sick, with an attack of fever, he turned over his stores to the Medical Director, Surgeon James C. Whitehill, and returned home.

In the meantime the Commission had forwarded additional supplies for this expedition, which were on the way to Helena, to be reshipped there up White river to Clarendon. Another agent, Mr. George M. Wyeth, who had been sent to Helena to act at that point, was now sent forward to take the place of Mr. Waterman. By the urgent advice of Surgeon Casselberry, Medical Director at Helena, he proceeded at once to join Gen. Steele's army at Duvall's Bluff, taking along the sanitary stores with him, which had previously arrived at Helena, and distributing them to the surgeons, for their sick, in general hospital, and to the regimental hospitals.

The army of Gen. Steele having advanced upon Little Rock, the capital of Arkansas, and after a battle with the rebel forces, under Gen. Price, captured the city, many sick were still left at Duvall's Bluff, where a general hospital had been established.

Better hospital accommodations, however, were found at Little Rock, which now had become the head-quarters of the Army of Arkansas, and the sick were soon removed and provided for there. Mr. Wyeth immediately established his agency at Little Rock, and distributed to the hospitals, and camps of the army, according to their necessities, receiving regular shipments of supplies from St. Louis, and fulfilling the duties of his position with fidelity and success.

Among the testimonials of the great good accomplished by this agency, a letter was received, September 30th, 1863, from Rev. E. S. Peake, Chaplain 28th Wisconsin Infantry, who had assisted Mr. Wyeth, in his work, in which he says:

"The Sanitary Commission has accomplished so much good by providing and forwarding supplies of the articles most needed for the relief and comfort of the sick in the Arkansas expedition, that it gives me great pleasure to send a brief statement of the facts. Your agent, Mr. Wyeth, arrived at Helena in time to learn the wants of the expedition, and followed the army up White river, to Duvall's Bluff, where our general hospital was established under temporary sheds. He brought some tons of sanitary stores, and remained there, attending to their proper distribution, until the order was given to remove all the sick to Little Rock. These supplies have been the means of saving many valuable lives to the army and to the country.

"Mr. Wyeth visited Little Rock by the first railroad train that came through, and took a tour of inspection through the hospitals, general and regimental, learning the actual condition of the sick, and their wants. He has sent to us all the supplies remaining at the Bluff, and has now gone to Helena, hoping to find another shipment from St. Louis at that point. The U. S. Sanitary Commission has sent its contributions to us through Dr. Fithian, so that we have been able to meet the call for aid, which comes from the hospitals of a large army, in a very satisfactory degree. We look upon this, however, as only the beginning in a great work of charity, which must be continued for several months to come.

"Let not our friends be weary in doing well. If they could see the good that they are doing, and the relief that their contributions afford, to the sick and wounded in the army, who, from their position, are helpless and dependent, it would prove an abundant encouragement and reward. The moral effect of this work upon the army is of great importance. It makes men braver and better soldiers and patriots, to see these tokens of interest, care, and love following them from their homes."

On the same day, Surgeon James C. Whitehill, medical director at Little Rock, also wrote to the President of the Commission:

"Permit me through Surgeon J. T. Hodgen to acknowledge the receipt of a fine supply of sanitary stores, and on behalf of our soldiers to thank you and the generous donors for so opportune a testimonial of their and your continued care and sympathy. We have had a great deal of sickness, and the country through which we have passed has been able to furnish but little adapted to the wants of the sick soldier. I have myself receipted to your agent, Mr. Wyeth, for the goods received, and placed them under the care of a most reliable and worthy man, who attends to their faithful distribution. Your Commission is doing an inconceivable amount of good for our sick soldiery· and deserves the hearty co-operation and liberal support of Christians and philanthropists."

During the summer the Commission had also sent a shipment of stores to the colored soldiers at Fort Blunt, in the Cherokee country, which was duly received and acknowledged by Surgeon S. C. Harrington, of the 1st Kansas Colored Infantry, in a letter, in which he says: "The goods were exceedingly opportune, as there was a great destitution of such things here. Were it not for your Commission, the army must suffer greatly for want of those things it most needs."

During the autumn of '63, generous supplies of sanitary stores were sent to the colored regiments, at Milliken's Bend, Goodrich's Landing, and Vicksburg. In a letter of Rev. Dr. Eliot, under date of August

21st, to friends in Boston, he wrote: "We have the whole army west of the Mississippi, to see to, and a large part of Gen. Grant's, and the gunboats, and the summer sickness are daily becoming worse. At Helena, where such grand fighting was done on the 4th of July, there are two thousand sick, left by armies moving forward. Gen. Steele writes, that he never needed our services more than now; and from every direction the claims come in upon us. We are making very large shipments daily, and are, this week, under the necessity of taking a large additional store-room for our bulky stores."

Under the same date, in answer to inquiries respecting colored troops, Mr. Yeatman writes: "We care for the sick and wounded colored soldiers, just as we do for the white. We have supplied a number of regiments in Louisiana, Mississippi, Kansas, and in this city. The accounts we have of them entitle them to our confidence."

During the fall and winter of 1863–4, Brig. Gen. Wm. A. Pile, organized three brigades of colored troops, at Benton Barracks, and in order that they might have every benefit that was possible, during the period of their organization and drill, the Commission purchased three thousand copies of Sargent's Standard Primer, for their use, and teachers were provided to instruct them in reading; their officers and Rev. Wm. H. Bradley, in the service of the Commission, taking part in this work. The sick of these brigades, in hospital, received the same treatment and attention as white troops; and sanitary stores were supplied, both from the Commission and from the Ladies Union Aid Society, as they were needed.

Among the acknowledgments received from the officers of colored troops, the following is given, from the colonel of the 1st Mississippi Vol. Infantry, A. D., dated:

"VICKSBURG, DEC. 29, 1863.

"REV. J. G. FORMAN,

"*Sec'ry Western Sanitary Commission:*

"DEAR SIR — I forward enclosed herewith, a receipt for sanitary stores, so kindly sent to my regiment. They will be of great benefit to my men, and I am very much obliged for so bountiful a supply. They will perform a great and needed good, not only for the sick, but for those on duty. I cannot but regard the prevention of disease, by suitable additions to the diet and comfort of the men, as important as it is to cure them, after they have filled the hospitals. I propose that my brave colored troops should have something extra on New Year's day.

"There is no limit to the good that can easily be done for this most susceptible people. How the minds of men have been blinded in regard to them! What outrageous sins has not our white humanity to account for! How dark blindness seems when one has passed from it to the broad light of day!

"The officers from the old 'Third Missouri' send their kindest regards.

"Yours, very truly,

"A. WATSON WEBBER,

"*Colonel Commanding.*"

During the fall and winter of 1863–4 generous supplies were sent by the Commission to the Nashville Branch of the Ladies' Union Aid Society, of St. Louis, and to Mrs. Barker, and other ladies, who were laboring in connection with the U. S. Christian Commission, both there and at Murfreesborough, Tenn., in the general hospitals. The long-tried and faithful agent of the Commission, Mr. A. W. Plattenburg, also went forward to Nashville with stores, and afterwards up the Tennessee river, as far as Eastport, to Gen. Sherman's army, and still later established an agency at Huntsville, Ala., from which point liberal supplies of sanitary goods have been furnished to the hospitals, and of vegetables to the troops, eliciting the warmest expressions of gratitude.

In a letter of Mr. Plattenburg, dated March 4th, 1864, he says:

"The vegetables sent by the Commission were issued *directly* to the soldiers, and a more thankful and pleased set of men has not been seen since the war."

This was at a time of great scarcity of vegetable food, and when the scurvy was making its appearance among the troops.

During the recent winter, supplies have also been furnished to the gunboats, and to the naval hospital steamer, "Red Rover." Among the goods sent were seventy-five libraries of books, one for each boat in the flotilla, and seventy-five sanitary store chests to the same number of vessels, each chest containing a good supply of hospital clothing, bandages, lint, adhesive plaster, condensed milk, farina, and other articles useful to the sick.

On the return of the veteran regiments of Missouri troops, on furlough, to return to the war for another three years, they have been received with a generous hospitality by the city of St. Louis, provided for at Turners' Hall, and escorted through the city by the Home Guards, with marked honor. Whenever they have needed any thing from the Sanitary Commission, as they went back to the army, it has been freely given. The veterans of Illinois, Iowa, and other States, have been treated in like manner, as regards their sanitary wants.

The 33d Illinois infantry, which had been stationed in Texas, and re-enlisted as veterans, on returning from their furlough, received from the Commission a sanitary chest, filled with excellent stores. The following acknowledgment was afterwards received, in which there are some of the reminiscences of the siege of Vicksburg given:

"HEADQUARTERS MEDICAL DEPARTMENT U. S. FORCES IN TEXAS,
"FORT ESPERANZA, MATAGORDA ISLAND, *Jan.* 15, 1864.

"REV. J. G. FORMAN,

"*Sec'ry Western Sanitary Commission:*

"MY DEAR SIR: Your timely supply of sanitary goods has been received, and in behalf of our noble soldiers, I would return to the Commission our grateful thanks for this and many other manifestations of kindness and interest in our sick and wounded men. I take pleasure in adding my testimony to that of many others, of the vast amount of good the Western Sanitary Commission has been instrumental in doing. I vividly remember the last 22d day of May, after the charge upon the fortifications of Vicksburg. Our division, (Gen. Carr's,) had about four hundred badly wounded men, brought into our division hospital on that day. We had been cut off from our base of supplies for over two weeks, had fought three successful battles, and had entirely exhausted all our medical and hospital stores. Our men were brought from the battle field with their winter clothing on, and in many cases their clothing and woolen blankets were saturated with blood, and covered with fly-blows, and we had no change to give them. We heard that communication was opened with Chickasaw Landing, twelve miles distant, and that a U. S. Government boat was there with supplies. At once, four wagons were sent there, with a request from the officer to send us the supplies that were so urgently needed, and the necessary papers could be executed afterwards. The wagons returned empty, and the men were told that nothing would be issued, unless the papers had gone through all the proper channels, and were tied with red tape, which would require several days to accomplish.

"One of the teamsters remarked to me, that he saw the boat of the Western Sanitary Commission, coming up the Yazoo river, as they were leaving. Our wagons were sent back, and our situation made known to that noble hearted gentleman, A. W. Plattenburg, agent of the Sanitary Commission, who at once loaded them with every thing necessary for the comfort and health of our wounded soldiers, and in a few hours a great change was seen in the hospital.

"The clothing was all changed, good beds were provided, nutritious food and proper stimulants prepared; and, but for this timely aid from your Commission, it is probable many of these poor soldiers would have died. This is only one instance. I could cite many others of a similar character, if time would permit.

"Go on in your noble efforts to ameliorate the condition of our unfortunate sick and wounded soldiers; and may God bless your efforts, and put it into the hearts of our loyal people to contribute still larger means to enable you to accomplish a greater amount of good.

"Very respectfully,

"GEORGE P. REX.

"*Surgeon 33d Illinois Infantry,*

"*Medical Director U. S. Forces in Texas.*"

A very large shipment of sanitary goods has also been sent this winter, to the army of Gen. Banks, on the Red river, and the Commission is at this date, (May 16th, 1864,) sending forward all the stores that can possibly be shipped to the army of Gen. Sherman, at Chattanooga, Dalton and Tunnel Hill, Georgia, to be prepared for the care of the sick and wounded of his army. Mr. H. E. Collins, its efficient and energetic agent, (late Cashier of the Commission,) is at Nashville, Tenn., pushing them forward, that no time may be lost, no pains spared, to meet any emergency that may arise. He will go on to Chattanooga, leaving Mr. Albert Clark at Nashville, to attend to future shipments. Mr. James Tompkins, another agent of the Commission, is now at Chattanooga, and will go forward to the front with his stores as soon as he can communicate with the Medical Director.

Having thus exhibited something of the work of the Western Sanitary Commission for the soldiers and sailors of the western armies and navy, there are several questions often raised, which may be appropriately answered here:

It is sometimes asked what need there is of Sanitary Commissions? Why don't the Government do this work, and take proper care of the soldiers, without depending on voluntary contributions? The answer is plain. The Government can only act through a system of regulations, by its authorized agents, who must be governed by prescribed rules and limitations, and held to a strict responsibility, or there would be no end to the waste and loss and imposition to which it would be subjected. Hence the necessity of a fixed ration for the soldier, and of supply tables for the hospitals, by which so much can be drawn and no more, the amount of hospital supplies being regulated according to the average number of sick. Thus it will often happen that the wants of an army in a time of sickness, or in an unhealthy locality, or after a battle, will greatly exceed the supplies on hand; and there is no way of meeting these emergencies, except through some such instrumentality as the Sanitary Commission.

In the army ration there is a deficiency of vegetable food. The amount of potatoes, for instance, to each ration, is not one-quarter of what would be a sufficient supply for a well man at home. In the hospitals it will barely answer for the hash that is given for breakfast, three times a week; and very often the proportion allowed to the well soldier is not given him, because the commissary has none. Sometimes for weeks and months, in the field, the regiments will receive no potatoes; and onions and other vegetables (still more rarely allowed) will be wanting. Such a want of vegetable diet soon engenders scurvy and other diseases that incapacitate the men for duty, and destroy life. To meet this want, the Western Sanitary Commission has forwarded many thousands of bushels of potatoes and onions, and thousands of cans of tomatoes, and kegs of pickles, to the army. And besides these supplies the surgeons in charge of hospitals make constant requisition for articles not furnished by Government, or not in sufficient quantity to meet the necessities of their patients.

Prejudicial stories have been circulated by many dissatisfied and fault-finding persons about the waste and consumption of sanitary stores by officers, accompanied by assertions that what is sent never reaches the private soldier. Much harm has been done in this way, by suspicious and evil-minded persons, discouraging contributions and preventing supplies from being sent to the army. In the early part of the war, before this great sanitary work had been reduced to a system, instances of waste and theft, and misappropriation of sanitary goods did no doubt sometimes occur; but even then they were the exception and not the rule. This evil has, however, been constantly diminishing; persons detected in it have been disgraced and dismissed from the service; and a greater degree of responsibility has been secured, with more ample means of exposure, so that now the misappropriation of sanitary goods can scarcely take place without bringing disgrace and punishment on the parties engaged in it.

Nevertheless, the impression still prevails with many that the private soldier never gets any of the sanitary stores sent to the army, and many soldiers themselves, who have received them in their hospital diet, and at the Soldiers' Homes, slept in comfortable beds, rested upon soft pillows, worn dressing-gowns, and socks, and slippers, in sick wards, and eaten vegetables, fruits, butter and delicacies at their meals, (not being informed of the fact) have never known that these things came from the Sanitary Commissions.

An interesting illustration of this is mentioned by Rev. Glen Wood, General Agent of the American Tract Society, who has spent much time in the army, in the distribution of reading matter. During a visit to a general hospital, which I think he said was at Murfreesboro' or Jackson, Tenn., he engaged in conversation with a convalescent soldier in one of the wards, who had just finished a letter to his wife. The soldier said to him:

"I received a letter from my wife, away in Wisconsin, and she writes that the Soldiers' Aid Society are getting up some sanitary stores to send to us, and that she is helping to make up a nice lot of things. I have just written to her, and told her not to do any such thing; that the soldiers never get what is sent to them; and that the surgeons and stewards and officers only feast on them, while the common soldiers get none."

Several of the other soldiers responded to the statement of their comrade, "That's so; we never see any sanitary stores here."

Rev. Mr. Wood said, "My dear sir, I think you must be mistaken. I have been through the army a good deal, and have seen a great many things received by the soldiers that were sent from home, through the Sanitary Commissions, and otherwise."

He continued, addressing the first speaker, "I see you have on a comfortable dressing-gown, and socks and slippers, and clean sheets, and a pillow on your bed; where did you get these things from ?"

"Well," said the soldier, "I reckon Uncle Sam fitted up this hospital, and these here articles came from the linen room."

Mr. Wood remarked again, "I noticed at dinner that you had potatoes, and pickles, and onions, and butter, and dried fruit, and tomatoes; where did you get these things from ?"

"O," said the former speaker again, "I reckon Uncle Sam provided 'em, or may be they were bought with the hospital fund."

"But," says Mr. Wood, "such things can scarcely be bought here for love or money. I don't see any in the market, and the sutlers ask a great price for them. Suppose we call in the steward, and see if he cannot throw some light on this question."

The steward was then requested to come in, and Mr. Wood asked him if he would be kind enough to state to these men where most of the articles of hospital clothing that had been mentioned, and the butter and fruit and vegetables, and other delicacies on the table, had come from.

"Why, boys," said the steward, "didn't you know we got those things from the Sanitary Commission ?"

Instantly the men dropped their heads in some confusion, and the first speaker replied, "No, sir, we didn't know it. Why didn't you tell us, and we shouldn't have said what we did to this gentleman. I hope he will excuse our mistake. As for me, I'm going to tear up my letter to my wife, (tearing it in pieces) and write her another, and tell her to go ahead with them sanitary stores, and right glad we shall be to get them."

The men seemed much pleased with this turn of affairs, and Mr. Wood left them, having made a most salutary impression, and giving them all the reading matter they wished.

There is no doubt that much harm has been done, by letters from men who are naturally croakers and fault-finders, in discouraging contributions to the Sanitary Commissions. The well soldier, who has always enjoyed his health, ought not, of course, to receive the delicacies and comforts designed only for the sick, and for hospital use. The vegetables distributed by the Commission he eats, without inquiring where they came from, and writes home that he has never received any thing from the Sanitary Commission.

The following method was adopted by Surgeon Charles H. Hughes, 1st Missouri State Militia, to cure one of these croakers of his fault-finding spirit. Surgeon Hughes stands very high in the esteem of those who know him, and his statement is worthy of all credit. He says in a letter to the Secretary, from De Soto, Mo., May 2d, 1864, acknowledging the receipt of sanitary stores:

"I will tell you how I cured a croaker in the St. Louis Hickory street hospital once. He said the steward got half the things sent by the Sanitary Commission. I took every thing from him, for a week, which had been furnished him by the Commission, his pocket comb, pocket handkerchief, slippers, socks, and gown, and reading matter. I deprived him of the looking-glass, feather pillow, and comforts, and, for the two latter, gave him a hard, hair pillow and Government blanket, and let him take his meals at a separate table, on the rations furnished by the commissary, and bought out of the fund. After that he croaked about the parsimony of Uncle Sam, and I put him in the guard-house. When he rejoined his company he was effectually cured.

"Much wrong has been done to the Sanitary cause, and to medical officers in the service, by the letters of these croakers. People are foolish enough to believe them, not knowing that the things which are usually sent to, and relished by the sick, are unwholesome, oftentimes, to the stomach of a healthy man, because they vitiate his appetite for the more substantial food which he most needs. A physician seldom indulges in sweetmeats, and the wearing apparel, hospital clothing, etc., sent by the Commission, always bear a stamp, which would disgrace any one but the legitimate wearer—the patriot soldier."

A strict accountability is maintained between the Western Sanitary Commission and all its agents in the field. Whenever stores are sent to the agents, they are forwarded by the United States quartermasters as Government freight, and they receipt for them, and are responsible for their delivery. When delivered to the agents of the Commission they receipt to the quartermasters, and the receipted bills of lading are returned to the chief quartermaster at St. Louis, and acknowledgments are also made to the Commission. When sanitary stores are distributed to the surgeons for the sick and wounded in hospitals, it is done in answer to written requisitions, and their receipts are taken and returned to the Commission at St. Louis. Piles of these documents are now on file at the Western Sanitary Commission rooms, and it can easily be shown what regiments and hospitals have received sanitary stores, and the use made of them, by the surgeons and stewards, inquired into.

The following General, Post, and Regimental hospitals are among the number that have been supplied by this Commission: New House of Refuge, St. Louis and City hospitals, General hospital, (corner of Fifth and Chesnut street,) Good Samaritan, Eliot, (Fourth street,) Pacific, Hickory street, Jefferson Barracks, Marine, Benton Barracks, Lawson and Small-pox hospitals, hospitals in Arnot's and Thornton & Pierce's buildings, Schofield Barracks and Military Prison; hospitals in Cairo, and Mound City, Ill.; at Paducah, and Columbus, Ky.; Pittsburg Landing, Union City, Jackson, Lagrange, Memphis, Nashville, and Murfreesboro', Tenn.; Corinth, and Vicksburg, Mississippi; Huntsville, Ala.; Helena, Clarendon, Brownsville, Duvall's Bluff, Fayetteville, Salem, and Little Rock, Ark.; Fort Blunt, Cherokee Nation; Young's Point, Milliken's Bend, Goodrich's Landing and Duckport, La.; hospitals of the 6th, 13th, 14th, 15th, 16th, and 17th army corps; and of Quimby's, Hovey's, Steele's, Logan's, McPherson's, Herron's, Kimball's, McArthur's, and Blair's divisions; and of Thayer's, Irving's, Wilder's, and the Marine brigade; hospitals at Otterville, Pacific

City, Rolla, St. Joseph, Sulphur Springs, Sedalia, Tipton, Commerce, St. Charles, Ironton, Pilot Knob, Cape Girardeau, Lebanon, Patterson, Jefferson City, Kansas City, Springfield, Mo.; Fort Scott, Fort Leavenworth, Kansas; Fort Halleck, Idaho; Evansville, Ind.; Quincy, Ill; and Keokuk, Iowa. Many stores were also issued to convalescent camps, and personally to large numbers of convalescent soldiers.

Among the regiments supplied, are all the Missouri troops, from the 1st to the 37th infantry; from the 1st to the 14th cavalry; Wellfly's and the other Missouri batteries of artillery; Bissell's engineer corps; Benton and Fremont Hussars, and Merrill's and Curtis' Horse; the Iowa troops, from the 1st to the 40th regiments of infantry; and the 1st, 2d, 3d, 4th, 5th, 6th, and 9th Iowa cavalry; and the 1st Iowa and Dubuque and Dodge's batteries; the 2d, 4th, 8th, 10th, 11th, 13th, 14th, 15th, 17th, 18th, 20th, 26th, 28th, 29th, 30th, 31st, 32d, 33d, 36th, 40th, 41st, 42d, 43d, 45th, 46th, 47th, 48th, 49th, 53d, 54th, 55th, 56th, 61st, 62d, 63d, 76th, 77th, 81st, 87th, 90th, 93d, 94th, 95th, 97th, 99th, 101st, 103d, 106th, 108th, 111th, 113th, 114th, 116th, 117th, 118th, 122d, 124th, 126th, 127th, 130th, 131st, 145th, and 147th Illinois infantry; the 5th, 6th, 7th, 9th, and 10th Illinois cavalry; and Peoria, Mercantile, Board of Trade, Taylor's, and 1st Illinois batteries; the 7th, 8th, 11th, 12th, 16th 18th, 23d, 24th, 25th, 34th, 39th, 43d, 47th, 48th, 49th, 53d, 54th, 56th, 59th, 60th, 67th, 72d, 83d, 93d, 96th, 97th, 99th, and 100th Indiana infantry; Coggswell's 1st Indiana battery; and the 1st Indiana cavalry; the 1st, 16th, 20th, 22d, 30th, 32d, 36th, 37th, 42d, 46th, 47th, 48th, 53d, 54th, 55th, 56th, 57th, 58th, 68th, 70th, 72d, 76th, 77th, 78th, 80th, 83d, 95th, 96th, 114th, and 120th Ohio infantry; 5th Ohio cavalry; and the 2d, 4th, 8th, 11th, 16th, and 26th Ohio batteries; the 1st, 2d, 6th, 8th, 9th, 11th, 12th, 14th, 16th, 17th, 18th, 23d, 25th, 27th, 28th, 29th, 32d, 33d, and 41st Wisconsin infantry; 12th Wisconsin battery; and 1st, 2d, and 3d Wisconsin cavalry; the 2d, 7th, 8th, 12th, 15th, 20th, and 27th Michigan infantry; and 2d and 3d Michigan cavalry; the 3d, 4th, 5th, 11th, and 17th Minnesota infantry; and 1st Minnesota battery; the 1st, 2d, 5th, 10th, 11th, and 13th Kansas infantry; and 1st and 5th Kansas cavalry; the 1st Arkansas, (white), 1st, 2d, 3d, and 4th Arkansas colored infantry; and the 1st, 3d, and 4th Arkansas cavalry; the 5th Maine infantry; the 11th New Hampshire infantry; the 32d Massachusetts infantry; the 17th and 178th New York infantry; the 34th and 35th New Jersey infantry; and 2d New Jersey cavalry; the 45th Pennsylvania infantry; the 4th Virginia infantry; the 7th, 19th, and 22d Kentucky infantry; the 8th, 9th, 10th, 11th, and 12th Louisiana colored infantry; the 1st, 2d, 3d, 4th, and 6th, Mississippi colored infantry; and 1st Mississippi colored cavalry; the 13th United States regular army; and the 48th, 49th, 51st, 58th, and 59th United States colored infantry; and 2d and 6th United States colored artillery.

The hospital steamers supplied by the Western Sanitary Commission, are the "*City of Louisiana*," afterwards refitted and named the "*R. C. Wood*," the "*D. A. January*," the "*Empress*," the "*Imperial*," the "*Red Rover*," the "*City of Alton*," the "*City of Memphis*," the "*Nashville*;" and of the transports, conveying the sick and wounded, the "*Ruth*," the "*Glasgow*," the "*Diana*," the "*Nebraska*," and the "*Baltic*."

Of the gunboats of the Mississippi naval squadron, supplies have been sent to nearly all, among which the following may be named: the *Louisville*, *Mound City*, *Carondelet*, *Chillicothe*, *Judge Torrence*, *Lafayette*, *Naumkeag*, *Ratler*, *Autocrat*, *Black Hawk*, *Petrel*, *General Price*, *Romeo*, *Choctaw*, *Benton*, *Avenger*, *Tyler*, *Monarch*, *Switzerland*, *Pawpaw*, *Tawha*, *Key West*, and *No.* 11, there being many more, to whom contributions have been sent quite recently, including the whole Mississippi squadron.

In concluding the present chapter, it is deemed an appropriate place to mention the names of those female nurses, who, by long and faithful service, and special devotion to the care of the sick and wounded soldiers, in the St. Louis hospitals, have earned the gratitude of the Western Sanitary Commission, and of those who have been the objects of their kind solicitude and self-sacrificing labors. In giving this list of honored names, it is not improbable that some will be omitted, who deserve a place in it, for it is made up under many disadvantages, and without all the means of a careful examination. It is also to be regretted that the Christian names of some are not within the knowledge of the writer, and cannot be easily obtained. The list is as follows: Mrs. M. I. Ballard, Mrs. E. O. Gibson, Mrs. L. D. Aldrich, Mrs. Houghton, Mrs. S. A. Plummer, Miss Carrie C. McNair, Mrs. Harriet Colfax, Mrs. Sarah A. Barton, Miss Ida Johnson, Miss Clark, Miss A. L. Ostram, Mrs. Lucy E. Starr, Mrs. Olive Freeman, Mrs. Anne M. Shattuck, Mrs. E. C. Brendell, Mrs. E. J. Morris, Mrs. Dorothea Ogden, Mrs. E. C. Witherell, Miss N. A. Shepherd, the Sisters of Charity at the New House of Refuge Hospital, Miss Emma L. Ingalls, Miss Emily E. Parsons, Miss Fanny Marshall, Miss Louisa Maertz, Miss Harriet N. Phillips, Mrs. Elizabeth A. Nichols, Miss Rebecca Craighead, Mrs. H. A. Haines, Mrs. H. A. Reid, Miss Hattie Wiswall, Mrs. Reese, Mrs. Maria Brooks, Mrs. Mary Allen, Mrs. Bickerdike, Miss Cornelia M. Tompkins, Mrs. M. A. Steller, Mrs. Carrie Gray, Mrs. M. J. Dykman, Misses Marian and Clara McClintock, Mrs. Otis, Mrs. Sager, Mrs. Peabody, Mrs. Rebecca S. Smith, Miss Melcenia Elliott, Mrs. C. C. Hagar, Mrs. J. E. Hickox, Mrs. Lucy L. Campbell, Miss C. A. Harwood, Miss Deborah Daugherty, Miss Phebe Allen, Mrs. Wells, Mrs. Ferris, and Miss Lucy J. Bissell.

Of these honored women, Mrs. E. C. Witherell laid down her life in this service. She had served very faithfully in the Eliot Hospital, St. Louis, for many months, and was always most gentle, kind, and unremitting in her attention to the sick and wounded. In the spring of 1862, she was transferred to the hospital steamer "*Empress*," as matron, and continued on her till the next July, when, on the 10th of the month she died, a victim of fever, contracted in performing the arduous duties of a nurse. The Western Sanitary Commission passed a preamble and resolutions, commemorative of her virtues, in which she was mentioned as one who was "gentle and unobtrusive, with a heart warm with sympathy, and unshrinking in the discharge of duty, energetic, untiring, ready to answer every call, and unwilling to spare herself where she could alleviate suffering, or minister to the comfort of others." In self-sacrifice and devotion to duty she was regarded as "not a whit behind the bravest hero on the battle field," giving, as she did, her life for her country and humanity.

If the history of the present war shall ever be faithfully written, it will contain many touching incidents of woman's heroism, and a noble record of the inestimable services rendered by her, in the hospitals of the army, living in an impure atmosphere, amid scenes of suffering and death, that the soldiers of the Union may be gently nursed and cared for, and sent forth again to do battle for a righteous cause. A young woman is now present to the mind of the writer, and her name is in the foregoing list, who came from her country home, in Iowa, a volunteer to nurse her country's defenders, among whom were all of her own brothers, who were old enough to fight. She had education, strength, and a holy resolution to undertake the hardest service she could find. For months she served in the hospitals of Tennessee, went home alone in charge of the corpse of a neighbor of her father's, who had died in the hospital at Memphis, returned to St. Louis, and when, in one of the large hospitals, a volunteer was called for, to serve in the erysipelas ward, a position of danger and of trying service, while others were reluctant, she made a ready and willing offer of herself, was accepted, and spent months in the cheerful performance of her duty there, without a murmur or complaint. She is still filling a position of arduous service and much responsibility, and may occasionally be seen, leading a blind soldier, in his visits to the surgeon, for the treatment of his eyes, taking delight in every opportunity of doing good to those who are giving their lives for their country.

Another one we also knew, whose name is likewise in this simple record, who, at Helena, Ark., in the fall and winter of 1862–3, was almost the only female nurse in the hospitals there, going from one building to another, in which the sick were quartered, when the streets were almost impassable with mud, administering sanitary stores, and making delicate preparations of food, spending her own money in procuring milk and other articles that were scarce and difficult to obtain, and doing an amount of work which few persons could sustain, living without the pleasant society to which she had been accustomed at home, never murmuring, always cheerful and kind, preserving in the midst of a military camp such gentleness, strength, and purity of character, that all rudeness of speech ceased in her presence, and, as she went from room to room, she was received with silent benedictions, or an audible "God bless you, dear lady, for your kindness to me," from some poor sufferer's heart.

When such women are willing to leave their pleasant homes, and forsake almost every comfort, for such a service, and in such a cause, there is still hope for the land of their birth ; for while virtue and self-sacrifice remain, the cause of liberty and free government cannot perish from the earth, but must grow stronger and more triumphant with every conflict, as ages roll away.

CHAPTER X.

THE FREEDMEN OF THE MISSISSIPPI—FIRST EFFORTS FOR THEIR RELIEF AT HELENA—MISS MARIA R. MANN—MR. YEATMAN'S VISITS TO THE FREEDMEN, FROM ISLAND NO. 10 TO NATCHEZ—CHAPLAIN H. D. FISHER DETAILED AS AN AGENT OF THE COMMISSION TO MAKE AN APPEAL FOR AID IN NEW ENGLAND—GENEROUS CONTRIBUTIONS RECEIVED—MR. YEATMAN'S REPORT—CONDITION OF THE FREEDMEN—THE SUBJECT PRESENTED TO THE ATTENTION OF THE GOVERNMENT—MR. W. P. MELLEN AND MR. YEATMAN RETURN TO CARRY INTO EFFECT AN IMPROVED SYSTEM OF LEASING THE ABANDONED PLANTATIONS, AND OF SECURING BETTER WAGES TO THE LABORERS—SECOND VISIT TO WASHINGTON—MILITARY PROTECTION GIVEN—NATIONAL AND OTHER FREEDMEN'S RELIEF ASSOCIATIONS—MESSRS. MARSH AND FOSTER GO TO VICKSBURG AS AGENTS—TEACHERS SENT—DEATH OF ONE OF THE NUMBER—FOUR THOUSAND FIVE HUNDRED FREEDMEN ARRIVE WITH THE RETURN OF GEN. SHERMAN'S ARMY FROM MERIDIAN—THEIR CONDITION—AID GIVEN—UNION REFUGEES OF THE MISSISSIPPI VALLEY—REFUGEE HOME AT ST. LOUIS—REFUGEES AT PILOT KNOB—LABORS OF SUPERINTENDENT A. WRIGHT—REFUGEE HOME AT VICKSBURG—SCHOOL FOR REFUGEE CHILDREN.

INCIDENTAL to its great work of ministering to the sick and wounded of the Western armies and navy, and of promoting the health and energy of our soldiers in the field, the Western Sanitary Commission has felt itself called to devote a portion of its labors to the relief of forty thousand freedmen, along the banks of the Mississippi river, from Columbus, Ky., to Natchez, many of whom, in their transition from the ownership and control of slave masters, to the condition of freedmen, have suffered untold hardships and privations, in a country stripped by the ravages of war, with no demand for labor, except in a few favored localities, nor any means of providing for their most urgent wants, food, clothing, and shelter. Seeing in them the victims of a life-long oppression, thrown destitute and almost naked upon the tender mercies of our armies in the field, many of them dying of exposure, hardship, and disease, the members of the Western Commission could not turn a deaf ear to their silent appeals for assistance and Christian sympathy.

Their attention was first called to the sufferings of these people at

Helena, in the beginning of the winter of 1862–3, where there were between three and four thousand, men, women and children, part of them living in a place back of the town, established for them, by Gen. C. C. Washburne, the previous summer, called "Camp Ethiopia," in the condemned and cast-off tents of the army, and in caves and shelters of brush—the best arrangement that could be made at the time, but wholly insufficient for winter. Others dwelt in the poorer houses of the town, sixteen and twenty persons occupying the same room, and others still in the few huts that remained on the neighboring plantations. The able-bodied men had been worked very hard on the fortifications of the place, and by the quartermasters, in unloading coal from barges and freight from steamboats, and also as grave-diggers, teamsters and wood choppers, and in all manner of fatigue duty. For these services many of them never received any compensation, through the neglect of the officers, having them in charge, to keep proper pay rolls, and the indifference of several of the military commanders, immediately succeeding Maj. Gen. Curtis. At one time an order was issued forbidding their payment, on the ground that their masters would have a claim against the Government for their services. All the while they were compelled to do most of the hard work of the place, and press-gangs were sent out to take them in the streets and put them to work, sometimes by night as well as by day, taking no account of their names or labor, and dismissing them without compensation. Sometimes they were shot down, and murdered with impunity.

Under such circumstances they were not able to provide for their families, and rations had to be drawn for them from the Government. Herded together as they were, in camps and the poorest dwellings, it was no wonder that they sickened and died at a fearful rate. The writer of this, who was then on duty at Helena, has seen the streets patroled by mounted orderlies, to gather up the "contrabands," as they were called, for forced labor, while their women and children were driven from their little houses, to Camp Ethiopa, under an arbitrary military rule, with a view of expelling them from the town; and there being no additional shelter at the camp, they had to suffer there, till the order became partially a dead letter, by reason of its inhumanity. A military order was as one time issued, to carry them beyond the lines, under which many of them were delivered up to rebel masters, in violation of the Articles of War. With hundreds of sick, their only hospital was a small building, not sufficient for the care of twenty persons.

It was under these circumstances, that the Western Sanitary Commission, early in January, 1863, sent to Helena, that excellent and philanthropic woman, Miss Maria R. Mann, with a large supply of sanitary stores, clothing, hospital goods, furniture, stove, &c., to fit up a better hospital for the sick of this class, and to minister generally to their wants.

At this time, Rev. Samuel Sawyer, chaplain of the 47th Indiana infantry, and Rev. J. G. Forman, chaplain of the 3d Missouri infantry, both of them on detached service at Helena, were doing what they could for these poor people, and welcomed the arrival of Miss Mann with great satisfaction. Mr. F. secured rooms for her and her stores in the same house occupied by himself and others, and the work of amelioration was immediately commenced. The hospital was soon renovated; and a month or two later, on the removal of a portion of the army, a larger and better building was obtained, when the sick of the freed people were better situated, and army surgeons were detailed to attend them. It was now known that a change of policy towards the emancipated people had been inaugurated by the Government. Adjutant General Thomas was on his way to look after these people, and organize regiments of fighting men from them, and the military commanders became more willing to grant favors in their behalf.

In the Spring a splendid regiment of the 1st Arkansas infantry, A. D., was recruited in a few days, commanded by Col. Wm. F. Wood, and a second was commenced. Miss Mann remained till the following August, performing a great amount of useful service to the wives and children of these men, giving clothing to the poor and needy, selling to those who had money to buy with, and replenishing her stock with the proceeds; teaching women to cut and make their own garments, providing medicines for the sick, visiting them in their camps and dwellings, giving them excellent advice, and in every possible way improving their condition.

Her labors there were also sustained by friends in New England, with whom she was in correspondence, and several thousand dollars worth of clothing, material for clothing, medicines, etc., were used by her in the most judicious manner, Rev. Dr. Eliot, at St. Louis, acting for the Commission, as Treasurer of a special fund for this purpose, contributed mostly by humane people in New England. Rev. Jonathan E. Thomas, chaplain 56th Ohio infantry, was also detailed to assist in this work, and his humanity and kindness to the poor "contrabands," as well as the faithful service of Rev. Mr. Sawyer, and the devoted labors of Miss Mann, will long be remembered by them, and by the writer of this sketch, who was providentially associated with them, for a time, in their benevolent work. It is due to Major Generals S. R. Curtis, C. C. Washburne, and Prentiss, who were in command at Helena for a brief period, to say that it was not during their administration of affairs that the evils here narrated occurred, and that they were always ready to do whatever was in their power, for the amelioration of the condition of the colored people at that post.

During the month of October, '63, the condition of the freed people, along the Mississippi river, again enlisted the earnest consideration of the Western Sanitary Commission. The same state of things that had existed at Helena, was reported as existing at many other points, between Columbus, Kentucky, and Natchez, chiefly the result of neglect, inability to procure remunerative employment, failure of quartermasters to enroll and pay the freedmen their wages, and the helpless condition of many, in consequence of the taking of the strong and able-bodied men for United States soldiers, leaving their wives and children, for a time, unprovided for.

On the 6th of November the Commission addressed a letter to the President of the United States, calling his attention to the condition of these people, the necessity of assistance, before another winter should set in, and proposing to assume the labor of soliciting contributions and extending relief, as an incidental part of its work. The proposal was favorably regarded, assurances were given by the Secretary of War that all possible aid would be rendered, in the way of transportation and otherwise, and, a few weeks later, Mr. Yeatman made a special visit down the river, to ascertain and report the actual state of things.

At the same time, Maj. Gen. Schofield, who gave his hearty approval and sympathy to the work, detailed, by special order, Chaplain H. D. Fisher, of the 5th Kansas Cavalry, to visit New England, under the direction of the Commission, and make a suitable appeal for contributions for this object. Mr. Fisher's visit was entirely successful, and very large contributions of clothing, material for clothing, shoes, and other necessary articles, amounting in value to about $30,000, and $13,000 in money, were obtained, by a committee in Boston, composed of Chas. G. Loring, *Chairman*, M. S. Scudder, *Secretary*, Alpheus Hardy, *Treasurer*, A. A. Lawrence, James M. Barnard, Wm. Endicott, Jr., Edward Atkinson, and sixteen others. These contributions came from Boston, Salem and other neighboring towns and cities, to whom the appeals of the Western Sanitary Commission have never been made in vain. Many valuable boxes of clothing material and shoes were sent by the Boston Educational Commission for Freedmen, of which Messrs. Barnard, Atkinson and Endicott, of the other committee, were also members.

On the 17th of December, Mr. Yeatman returned from his first visit to the freedmen of the lower Mississippi, and made a full report to the Commission, of which five thousand copies were printed and circulated. He stopped at Island No. 10, at Memphis, Helena, Goodrich's Landing,

Milliken's Bend, Young's Point and Vicksburg, the plantations of Jeff and Joe Davis, and at Natchez, and returning, visited some of these points a second time.

The report, consisting of sixteen pages of closely printed matter, is so full of information that it is impossible to make even an abstract of it for this work. It is sufficient to say, that he found about forty thousand of these people in camps, at the above and other places, between Cairo and Natchez, in various degrees of poverty and wretchedness; that among them he found several volunteer agents, missionaries, and teachers, from the United Presbyterians, the Friends, and the Freedmen's Aid Associations, laboring for their benefit as well as they could, without system or co-operation; that in the cotton growing region, from Goodrich's Landing to Vicksburg, on the abandoned plantations, leased by the Government, he saw over twenty colored men, and heard of others who had raised from five to ten bales of cotton, on their own account, proving their capacity for self-maintenance, with a fair chance; that where they were laboring under the lessees their wages were wholly inadequate, being but five dollars per month for women, and seven dollars per month for men, with subsistence of the poorest kind; that they suffered many wrongs under this system; that when they were employed by Government Quartermasters, to cut wood for steamboats, they were frequently not paid ; that they were charged an unreasonable price for goods, and were really suffering wrongs and hardships, equal to those they had borne in a state of slavery, while they were enjoying none of the blessings of liberty.

Mr. Yeatman, in his report, thus sets forth some of the wrongs of these people: "Within the city of Memphis, not directly connected with any of the camps, or with the colored regiments, there are some *three thousand* freed men and women, mostly freed men, who are employed in various ways, and at various rates of compensation. Those employed by Government, receive but ten dollars per month, while many could readily earn from thirty to fifty dollars per month. Those thus employed are outside of the military organization.

"To give an instance: One quartermaster told me that he had in his employment, a harness maker, to whom he could only pay ten dollars per month, while he was paying white men, doing the same work, forty-five dollars per month; and that the colored man could readily procure the same wages, were he allowed to seek a market for his labor in the same town. I saw a number of colored men pressed into service, (not military,) to labor at the rate of ten dollars per month, one of whom petitioned to be released, as he had a good situation at thirty dollars per month. The firemen on the steamboat on which I was a passenger from St. Louis to Memphis, were all colored, and were receiving forty-five dollars per month. These men were afraid to go ashore at Memphis, for fear of being picked up and forced into Government employment, at less than one-fourth their existing wages.

"Besides the fact that men are thus pressed into service, thousands have been employed for weeks and months, who have never received any thing but promises to pay. This negligence and failure to comply with obligations, have greatly disheartened the poor slave, who comes forth at the call of the President, and supposes himself a free man, and that, by leaving his rebel master, he is inflicting a blow on the enemy, ceasing to labor and to provide food for him and for the armies of the rebellion. Thus he was promised freedom, but how is it with him? He is seized in the street, and ordered to go and help unload a steamboat, for which he will be paid, or sent to work in the trenches, or to labor for some quartermaster, or to chop wood for the Government. He labors for months, and at last is only paid with promises, unless perchance it may be with kicks, cuffs, and curses.

"Under such treatment, he feels that he has exchanged one master for many masters; these continued abuses sadden and depress him, and he sighs to return to his former home and master. He, at least, fed, clothed, and sheltered him. Something should be done, and I doubt not, will be done, to correct these terrible abuses, when the proper authorities are made to comprehend them. The President's proclamation should not thus be made a living lie, as the Declaration of Independence has too long been, in asserting the inalienable rights of man, while the nation continued to hold millions of human beings in bondage."

In another place he says :

"The poor negroes are everywhere greatly depressed at their condition. They all testify that if they were only paid their little wages as they earn them, so that they could purchase clothing, and were furnished with the provisions promised, they could stand it; but to work and get poorly paid, poorly fed, and not doctored when sick, is more than they can endure. Among the thousands whom I questioned, none showed the least unwillingness to work. If they could only be paid fair wages, they would be contented and happy. They do not realize that they are free men. They say that they are told they are, but then they are taken and hired out to men who treat them, so far as providing for them is concerned, far worse than their "secesh" masters did. Besides this they feel that their pay or hire is lower now than it was when the "secesh" used to hire them. This is true."

And yet, under all their accumulated wrongs, these people manifest a wonderful faith in Divine Providence; they seem to be sensible that God has some better thing in store for them, and to realize that, through this wilderness of suffering and sorrow is the only path to their deliverance. Mrs. Porter, at Camp Holly Spring, near Memphis, related to Mr. Yeatman an instance of this. When she first went there to teach, an old negro came out to meet her, whose head had been whitened by the frosts of ninety winters, and who was almost blind, supporting himself by his staff. With his hand stretched forth he accosted her, saying, "Well, you hab come at las'. I'se been 'spectin' you, lookin' for you, for de las' twenty years. I knowed you would come, and now I rejoice." She said, "I have come to teach you." "Yes, yes, I know it, and I tank de Lord."

At this same camp Mr. Yeatman saw a colored man, who, after his return from his work, was seated in his cabin, surrounded by his own children and a few others from the adjoining cabins, teaching them their lessons for the morrow. At another school he met an old woman, aged eighty-five, who was intent on her books. When asked if she was not too old to begin to learn, she said, "No," that she must learn now or not at all, as she had but little time left, and she must make the most of it. When asked what good it would do her, she said "she could read de bible, and teach de young." At other places similar instances of faith and piety, and the desire of knowledge, were witnessed.

Mr. Yeatman was most favorably impressed with the capacity of the negroes to become soldiers. He gives an account of several successful expeditions, under Col. Farrar, at Natchez, in which they brought in prisoners. In one instance he says, "The prisoners were much chagrined at being taken by negroes, and asked if they could not have another guard to take them through town; but as they were captured by negroes, they had to be guarded and escorted by them."

He says of another experience he had, "In going from Goodrich's Landing to Milliken's Bend, I was escorted by twenty colored troops, mounted on mules captured from the enemy. They rode gallantly and fearlessly, putting our their advance guard and arranging themselves in true military order, conducting themselves with as much propriety as an equal number of well behaved gentlemen. When we arrived at the Bend, and dashed into the fort, surrounded by troops, my companion—Dr. May—and myself, dressed in citizen's clothes, and mounted in an old wagon, were taken for prisoners, and our escort was called out to by the soldiers, "Rebs! Rebs!" and an amount of ivory displayed that I have seldom seen exceeded.

"I could but compare my first visit to this point years ago, when I landed to take charge of a large estate, as executor, with my present one. It was here in these swamps that I first saw and knew what a dead, leaden thing slavery is, and the wrong and injustice which could be inflicted, even by one, considered the kindest and most humane of masters. I doubt not the seed was then sown in my heart which has since germinated, and makes me now not only willing, but anxious to labor for these poor sons of soil. What a revolution a few short years has brought about! Who can doubt that an infinitely wise and just God governs the world?"

On submitting his report to the Commission, Mr. Yeatman was delegated to visit Washington, and present this subject to the Government. In doing so, he also presented a series of printed "suggestions of a plan of organization for freed labor and the leasing of plantations along the Mississippi river." His report and suggestions were most favorably received at Washington, and he was urged and authorized to accompany Mr. W. P. Mellen, the special supervising agent of the Treasury Department, to Vicksburg, to mature and carry them into effect. This trust of the Government he accepted, as a voluntary work, declining an official position, which was offered him; and he proceeded a second time, now in company with Mr. Mellen, to the region of the leased plantations, near Vicksburg.

The new plan of labor—in view of the high price of cotton, and the profit to be derived from its cultivation—provided that the freedmen should receive from $12 to $25 a month, according to age, sex, abilitv, etc.; that there should be a secure method of enforcing the contract for labor and wages; that the lessee should furnish goods at an advance of ten per cent. on the cost; that there should be established "Home Farms," under a superintendent, for the young and old, the infirm and destitute; that there should be schools and teachers, for all children under twelve years old; and that a tax should be paid to the Government of four dollars, on each bale of cotton raised, and of two cents per pound, for the support of the "Home Farms," and the schools; and that the system should be carried out by commissioners of plantations, acting under the Treasury Department, who should see that justice is administered; that the freed people are treated as free, and encouraged to respect and observe the institutions of religion, marriage, and all the customs of virtuous and civilized society, and to become worthy of the blessings of a Christian civilization.

On their way down the river, Messrs. Mellen and Yeatman had a new form of lease, and printed regulations prepared at Memphis, and on arriving at Vicksburg, inaugurated the new order of things. At first it met with some opposition from the old lessees, who saw in it a diminution of their gains; but seeing that it was promulgated with authority, it was acquiesced in, local agents were appointed, and about six hundred plantations were immediately leased, under the new system.

The withdrawal of the troops, from some of the districts, had caused considerable discouragement at first, but on a second visit of Messrs. Mellen and Yeatman to Washington, the Secretary of War was induced to give the services of the Marine Brigade, for the purpose of affording protection to the plantations and freed people; and the work of growing cotton, the present year, is already progressing with satisfaction to all concerned, with a great improvement in the prospects of the laborers, and their ultimate success as independent cultivators of the soil; for the more intelligent of them do not fail to see the advantages of possessing land of their own, and are ambitious to work for themselves, instead of a master. In almost every instance where they attempted, last year, to cultivate cotton, on their own account, they were entirely successful, numerous instances of which Mr. Yeatman gave in his published report.

While these changes were being effected, a National Freedman's Relief Association had been organized in New York city, and a Northwestern Freedmen's Relief Commission at Chicago, besides which there were two similar associations already existing at Cincinnati, and another was formed at Indianapolis, Harmonious relations were at once established between these Associations and the Western Sanitary Commission.

On the 11th December, Messrs. Wm. L. Marsh and H. R. Foster, from the National Freedmen's Relief Association of New York, arrived at St. Louis, with a letter of introduction from Hon. F. G. Shaw, the President of the Association, on their way to Vicksburg, to establish an agency there, for the distribution of goods to the needy, the sale of them to those who could pay, and for the employment of teachers to instruct the people. Mr. Yeatman was at the time down the river; but these gentlemen, seeing the advantages of co-operation and unity of purpose, consented to act also as agents of the Western Sanitary Commission, and thereby secured an arrangement for the re-shipment of their goods from St. Louis to Vicksburg, which they were expecting from New York, and the Commission also secured the benefit of their valuable services, as agents in the field.

Very large shipments of clothing soon began to arrive from New York, directed to Mr. Marsh, and were forwarded with shipments from the Western Sanitary Commission, at the earliest period. They were unfortunately delayed several weeks by the severe cold of December and January, which closed the navigation for awhile, but were ultimately received, and accomplished great good. Of the proceeds of the goods sold by these gentlemen, on account of the Western Sanitary Commission, they have returned $1000. Their services have been in every respect most useful and satisfactory, and have been extended to Natchez, and other places besides Vicksburg.

During the winter they wrote to the Commission to send them two teachers, to assist in the work of instruction and distribution at Vicksburg. Miss A. M. Knight, of Sun Prairie, Wis., and Miss Sarah J. Hagar, of this city, were commissioned, and their services have been very acceptable and useful. In February, Mrs. Lydia H. Daggett, of Boston, a very excellent and capable person, was sent into the same field, to act under the direction of Mr. Marsh.

Within a few days, the friends of Miss Hagar have been pained to receive the news of her unexpected death, at Vicksburg, from a sudden attack of disease. She was a devoted, and estimable young woman. It is due to her memory, that the following letter, from Mr. Marsh, should have a place here, since she died in the service of the Commission, and in so good a cause.

"NATCHEZ, *May* 6, 1864.

"REV. J. G. FORMAN,

"*Sec'ry Western Sanitary Commission:*

"MY DEAR SIR—You have already received from Mr. Mann, the sad intelligence of the death of Miss Hagar, one of the teachers sent by you, to labor among the freed people in this valley.

"I was at Natchez when she was taken ill, and did not receive intelligence of it in time to reach Vicksburg, until after her death, which occurred on Tuesday, May 3d.

"In her death, the Association have lost a most *earnest*, devoted and Christian laborer. She entered upon her duties at a time of great suffering and destitution, among the freedmen, at Vicksburg, and when we were much in need of aid. The fidelity with which she performed her labors, and the deep interest she manifested in them, soon endeared her to us all. We shall miss her sorely; but the noble example she has left us, will encourage us to greater efforts and more patient toil. She seemed to realize the magnitude and importance of the work upon which she had entered, and the need of Divine assistance, in its performance. She seemed also to realize what sacrifice *might be* demanded of one engaged in a work like this, and the summons, although sudden, did not find her unprepared to meet it. She has done a noble work, and *done it well.* The sacrifice she made, is the greatest one that can be made for any cause, the *sacrifice of life.* 'Greater love than this, hath no man; that a man lay down his life for his friends.' She has gone to receive her reward.

"The family thus suddenly bereaved, and plunged in affliction, by this sad occurrence, has our sympathies and prayers. When they meet to perform the last sad rites due to the dead, may they not look in the close, narrow, burial-case for their loved one, but rather raise their eyes to behold a spirit, freed from earthly fetters, clothed in spotless robes, and wearing the crown bestowed only upon those who prove faithful to the end. Respectfully,

"W. L. MARSH."

Besides the labors of Messrs. Marsh and Foster at Vicksburg, the regular agent of the Commission, Mr. N. M. Mann, has taken a deep interest in the same work, and though much occupied in the superintendence of the Soldiers' Home, and the care of the refugees, he has found time to lend a helping hand. An interesting letter was received from him, dated the 7th of March, in which he gives a full account of the arrival of the four thousand five hundred freedmen, who returned with Gen'l Sherman's Army, from Meridian, and of his distributions of food and clothing among them. "Anticipating a need," he says, "I had drawn heavily on the Commissary for bread and had a large amount on hand. I had the ambulance of the Western Sanitary Commission loaded with this bread, and taking along half a dozen kind-hearted soldiers, we went the whole length of this wagon train and gave to each family a loaf or two. It was but a little thing to do, but the eagerness with which they took and ate it told how grateful it was to them. I assure you I never was more happy than that night, amid all that wretchedness, giving bread to those hungry creatures. That night they lay on the levee, in their wagons, and on the ground. Many who came from plantations this side of Jackson were without conveyances, having walked in, bearing their "effects" on their heads. The next morning they were sent on Steamboats to camps at Davis' Bend, and Oswego Landing, and in company with Mrs. Harvey, of Wisconsin, and Miss Dart, a teacher from New England, I went to Oswego with a quantity of old clothing, furnished by the National Freedmen's Relief Association, of New York, for distribution. To all the most destitute, or rather the most torn and naked, for all are destitute, we gave some of the more necessary articles of clothing. I only wish that the donors of those articles could have witnessed the distribution. I do not know where on the face of the globe, out of the Southern Confederacy, a thousand people could be got together that would present to charity so strong an appeal as these. I wish I could send to every Northern home of plenty, a photograph of these bare-footed, ragged, half-naked creatures, as they appeared to me that day. They had been fed, and although their destitute, filthy, tattered and homeless condition was enough to draw tears from a heart of stone, many were cheerful and gave evidence that, with a very little comfort, they would be happy. The endurance of the negro has always been a marvel. It was never so much so as now. It is his difference from the white man, in this respect, that is to save him, if he is saved, in this great trial."

The Union refugees have also received a share in the labors of the Western Sanitary Commission. During the fall and winter of 1861–2 many refugees were driven, by the rebels, from the interior and south-west parts of Missouri to St. Louis, and were in a condition of want and suffering. A home, on Elm street, was opened for the most helpless and destitute, and others were assisted, according to their necessities. Mr. John Cavender, an old and respectable citizen, eminent for his integrity and christian character, devoted his whole time to their care. A fund was raised at first, by a call of the Western Sanitary Commission, amounting to about $3,800, besides a large amount of clothing. A further sum of $15,000 was raised by an order of Maj. Gen. Halleck, by assessing the wealthy class of secessionists, in St. Louis, for this object, and from this resource Mr. Cavender was able to render very important aid to these persecuted and destitute people. For two years he took almost the entire charge of this work, in which he had the counsel of the members of the Commission, and was sometimes aided with funds for the purpose, when other sources failed. During the winter of 1863, Mr. Cavender, whose health had been failing, was taken sick and died, and there was but little demand from that time, till the next

September, for any further aid to the refugees. In this charitable service no one could have been more faithful and constant than Mr. Cavender had been; and in other relations and duties, during an honorable and well spent life, he had been distinguished as the upright citizen, and patron of christian learning and philanthropy, and his death was greatly lamented.

In August, '63, there began to be further arrivals of destitute refugees from Arkansas, Tennessee, Mississippi, Alabama, Louisiana, and Texas. Many of them were women, with small children, poorly clad, often barefooted, brought up the river on Government steamers, and landed here, without the means of procuring a place of shelter for a single night. Their husbands had been killed in the war, had been murdered by guerrillas, had been conscripted into the rebel army, or had died from the effects of exposure in lying out in the woods, in dens and caves of the earth, to escape the blood-hounds of the rebel conscription. At first these poor refugee families fell into the hands of the police but the police station was not a fit place for them, although some of them found shelter there.

One day, late in August, the President of the Commission was called to see what could be done for a poor blind woman, and her family of six children, who had walked all the way from Arkansas to Rolla, Mo., her little children leading her several hundred miles by the hand, and from Rolla they had been brought on the cars to St. Louis, as a charity. They were in an upper unfurnished room of the Pacific hotel, the woman, and a boy about twelve years old, being sick, and she totally blind. They sat upon the floor, clothed in rags, and presented a sight that would have moved the stoutest heart to pity and to tears.

The children of this woman, whose name was Mrs. Hargrave, were adopted by Rev. Dr. Eliot, and placed in the Mission school on Eighth street, and the mother was sent to the St. Louis hospital, kept by the Sisters of Charity. Her youngest children she had never seen, they having been born since she became blind. The parting of the blind mother from her little ones was a touching scene. But she gave them up willingly, knowing it to be a necessity, and for their good. At the Sisters' hospital, her health, after several months, was restored, and, by a surgical operation of Dr. Pope, the cataracts were removed from her eyes, and she was able to see. Her children were then brought to her, and the meeting can be better imagined than described.

A little later, another refugee mother came, and, with two little children, stood at the door of the Commission, on Fifth street, having no place to go. They were barefooted, dusty with travel, and miserably clad. The mother told her sad story.

Her husband had been murdered by guerrillas, near Fort Smith, Ark., and she had walked, with her children, to Rolla, riding part of the way in Government wagons, and had reached St. Louis, as a place of refuge. She had to stay at the police station that night. The next day, three women and children arrived from Jackson, Tenn., in an equally destitute condition. There was no alternative but to open another refugee home. The President of the Commission rented the house, 39 Walnut street, for the purpose, on the 1st of September, and from that date to the present, not less than fifteen hundred refugees have been sheltered, provided for, or sent on their way to friends, or places of employment, in the free States. By an arrangement with Generals Schofield and Rosecrans, rations and fuel are allowed from the Government, and the rent is paid by the Quartermaster; but the incidental expenses of the home, and the charities in clothing, money, &c., are provided by the Commission. It is under the superintendence of Rev. Mr. Forman, the Secretary of the Commission, and its domestic arrangements are conducted by Miss M. Elliott, as Matron, who, in a spirit of true self-sacrifice, devotes her time and strength to the service of these poor outcasts from the rebellion. The expenses and charities of the Home, and for destitute refugee families in the city, and to those going beyond St. Louis, have been about $1,000 in six months, beyond the aid received from the Government in rations, fuel, rent, and transportation. Several valuable boxes of clothing have been received from New England; also contributions of money from Boston, from the Ladies' Loyal League, of St. Louis, and from various other sources. The receipts for this charity and for the Freedmen, and the disbursements are kept separate from the other funds and resources of the Commission, so that there is no misappropriation of what is designed for the soldiers to these objects. Contributors are always requested to designate the object of their charities, and if no designation is made, they go into the sanitary fund.

The number of refugees at Pilot Knob, at the present time, is over 1700 persons, mostly women and children. They are chiefly from Arkansas, and are under the superintendence of a faithful and excellent man, Chaplain A. Wright, who has been specially assigned to that duty. Contributions to the value of several thousand dollars in goods, clothing, shoes, medicines for the sick, hardware and sash to assist in building cheap houses, and over $1000 in money have been sent to Mr. Wright, and expended in a judicious manner. At a time of special distress the Commission sent him fifteen barrels of clothing, eighty dollars in material for clothing, (purchased by Mrs. General Fisk) twenty dollars in money, sixty dollars in medicines, thirty dollars worth of glazed sash, half a dozen axes for women, who cut their own wood; and of the other contributions a large portion was collected by Mrs. Fisk, who made visits to Pilot Knob, and was most energetic and successful in her endeavors to relieve and benefit these poor people. Brig. Gen. Fisk, also, while commanding the District, did every thing in his power to minister to their wants.

The Western Commission also responded to an appeal from Mr. J. R. Brown, agent U. S. Sanitary Commission at Leavenworth City, for aid to refugees at that post, and at Fort Scott, Kansas, and sent thirty boxes of clothing to those points, and a thousand Union Spellers for schools of the freed children at Leavenworth.

At Rolla, Springfield, Cape Girardeau, Cairo, Columbus, Memphis,

Helena, and Vicksburg, there are multitudes of these poor refugees, numbered by thousands, who have come to us from rebel persecution and outrage, or have been driven, by the ravages of war, and the destitution of food and clothing, to seek a refuge within our lines. Humanity requires that they should be aided, at least to the extent of saving life, and to enable them to reach places, where employment and subsistance can be found.

Recently a necessity has arisen for a Refugee Home at Vicksburg, and the Commission has established one there, under the superintendence of Mr. Mann, with Mrs. Maria Brooks for matron. It was opened on the 1st of April, and has already received and aided 2,160 of these poor people. On the 7th of May, there were 620 remaining, mostly women and children. Transportation had been furnished to those wishing to emigrate North, and employment for the able-bodied men.

The large number of destitute white children, belonging to these families, having no means of instruction, has induced the Commission to send a teacher, Miss G. C. Chapman, to Vicksburg, to open a school for them, in connection with the Home, also under Mr. Mann's superintendence. This lady is now on her way, with a supply of school books for this purpose.

In all these enterprises of benevolence, Mr. Mann, as the agent of the Commission, has had the sanction, advice and co-operation of General McArthur, commanding at Vicksburg, who has assigned to the Commission suitable buildings for the purpose, and shown his great friendliness in this and many other ways.

CHAPTER XI.

Resources of the Western Sanitary Commission — Appropriations by the Governor and Legislature of Missouri — Liberality of St. Louis – Donations from Massachusetts and California — Gifts of the People — Contributions from the Women of the Loyal States — Distributions by the Commission — Number of Articles given — Estimated value, one and a half millions of dollars — Expenses of the Commission for Salaries of Agents, Rents, and Distribution of Stores less than one per cent. — Friendship of Major Generals Fremont, Halleck, Curtis, Schofield, Rosecrans, Sherman, and Lieut. Gen. Grant for the Commission — Also, of Assistant Surgeon General Wood, Gen. Allen, Colonels Parsons, Myers, Haines, and Maj. Smith — Ladies Union Aid Society of St. Louis — Its Work — Receipts and Disbursements — Freedmen's Relief Society of St. Louis — Its Work — Receipts and Disbursements — Mississippi Valley Sanitary Fair — Conclusion.

The resources of the Western Sanitary Commission have consisted of the voluntary contributions of the people of the loyal States. Noble men and women in the leading towns and citizens of New England, in the great Northwest, and in a few of the great cities of the seaboard—Boston, Providence, New York, and Philadelphia—have for nearly three years given liberally of their means and influence to strengthen this Commission, and help it to do the work which Providence has given it to do.

But, beside all these, the city and county of St. Louis, and the Legislature of Missouri, have acted with a generosity and patriotism worthy of all honor. In addition to the liberal contributions of the citizens, during the first year of the labors of the Commission, the late Gov. Gamble, from an appropriation by the Convention of Missouri, for the benefit of Missouri troops, placed $50,000 in the treasury of the Commission, to be used for sick and wounded soldiers of the State of Missouri. This sum was used, not by singling out that class of soldiers for special care, but caring for all United States soldiers alike, an account was kept of the extent to which Missouri troops shared in these benefits, and the amount, being far beyond the appropriation, the State authorities were abundantly satisfied and pleased with the use made of these funds.

Again, in the winter of 1864, the Legislature of Missouri made another appropriation of $25,000 to the Commission, to be used in the same way, and the county court of the county of St. Louis made a donation of $2,000. Besides these gifts, there was raised, at the Merchants' Exchange, St. Louis, a liberal subscription of money and goods to the Commission, for the army of Gen. Grant, during the siege of Vicksburg, amounting in value to about $5,000, and December 25th, 1863, a committee of the merchants, of which Mr. Joseph C. Cabot was chairman, raised another subscription of $25,000 additional, for the general purposes of the Commission.

Besides a constant flow of contributions from Boston and neighboring towns and cities of Massachusetts, that city at one time, through a committee, of which R. C. Greenleaf was treasurer, in response to an appeal from Rev. Dr. Eliot, on behalf of the Commission, contributed $50,000; and the distant State of California, stimulated by the eloquence and patriotism of the lamented Thomas Starr King, subscribed $50,000, being part of a donation of $200,000, the balance of which went to the United States Sanitary Commission. These contributions of money, with the gifts of friends in New York city, through that noble and patriotic citizen, James A. Roosevelt, and from other towns and cities of the loyal States, have amounted in the aggregate, to $275,000 in money; while the stores contributed from the same sources, and from the Ladies' Union Aid Societies, of almost every village and city from Maine to Minnesota, and from Boston to St. Louis, consisting of blankets, comforts, sheets, pillows, pillow-slips, socks, slippers, mittens, bandages, lint, salves, cotton and woolen shirts and drawers, hospital garments, dressing gowns, dried and canned fruits, tomatoes, jellies, domestic wines, blackberry cordials, butter, vegetables, pickles, books, reading matter, and thousands of other useful articles, have amounted in value to more than a million and a quarter of dollars.

Out of these contributions, the Commission has issued to the western armies, 985,984 articles; 28,838 to the western navy; 80,505 to freedmen, and 5,848 to Union refugees, making an aggregate of 1,101,174 articles.

In addition to these, many thousands of articles were given out during the first three months of the labors of the Commission, that no account was made of; and we have reason to believe, that many thousand more have escaped entry; it is so difficult, in the hurry occasioned by a great battle, or a pressing emergency, to keep an accurate record. During the months of June, 1863, and February, '64, the distributions of the Commission reached 184,333 articles. These, it is true, were busy months, but not more so than those which succeeded the battles of Fort Donelson, Pea Ridge, and Pittsburgh Landing. During the first nine months of the labors of the Commission, its records show a distribution of over 250,000 articles, so that we are quite confident of a large under estimate in the statistics here given, but they accord with the books, and we are not willing to make any exaggerations. The expenses of the Commission, during the whole period of its labors, for the salaries of agents, employees, rents, etc., is less than one per cent. of the whole amount distributed. The services of the members of the Commission, which includes the President and Treasurer, are gratuitous.

Through all this immense labor, from September 5th, 1861, to the present date, the Commission has enjoyed the friendly confidence and co-operation of every commander of the Department; and to Major Generals Fremont, Halleck, Curtis, Schofield, and Rosecrans, to the Secretary of War, and to Lieut. Gen'l Grant, and Maj. Gen'l Sherman in the field, it is much indebted for their support, and the facilities it has enjoyed in the transportation of supplies, in letters of commendation, in access to the armies, in the respect paid to it by surgeons and subordinate officers, and in varied opportunities of usefulness. To Assistant Surgeon General R. C. Wood, Gen. Robert Allen, Colonels L. B. Parsons, and William M. Myers, of the Quartermaster's Department; to Col. Haines and Capt. King of the Commissary Department, and to Maj. Robert Smith, of the Pay Department, the Commission is indebted for many favors, and for obliging and gentlemanly treatment on all occasions.

The names of contributors to the funds and stores of the Commission, it would be a pleasure to record here, yet their number is so great, and the space allotted to this work already so nearly filled, that the writer is not able to do them this honor; but their names are registered, in the Lamb's Book of Life, recorded by the angels in Heaven, and they shall all be known and recognized in the resurrection of the just.

Before concluding this work, it remains to give a brief account of two co-operative associations in St. Louis: the Ladies' Union Aid Society, and the Freedmen's Relief Society, and to notice the Mississippi Valley Sanitary Fair, now in successful operation, while these concluding pages are being written—an enterprize inaugurated for the benefit of the cause in which the Western Sanitary Commission, and these kindred associations, are engaged.

The Ladies' Union Aid Society of St. Louis was organized August 2d, 1861. Mrs. C. W. Stevens was the first President. Its officers at present are, Mrs. Alfred Clapp, President, Mrs. Saml. C. Davis, Mrs. T. M. Post, and Mrs. Robert Anderson, Vice-Presidents; Mrs. S. B. Kellogg, Treasurer; Miss H. A. Adams, Recording Secretary, and Miss Belle Holmes, Corresponding Secretary. Miss A. S. Debenham and Miss S. F. McCracken have also acted as Secretaries in the absence of the regular Recording Secretary, for several months, at Nashville, Tennessee.

The friendly connection and co-operation of this association with the Western Sanitary Commission has already appeared in the course of these pages, and want of space now precludes a full statement of its separate work, which has been already made public in a valuable report of forty-eight pages for the year 1863.

The work of the society has consisted in hospital visiting, in aid to soldiers' families, in the distribution of religious reading, from the Christian Commission, in volunteering as nurses after the great battles, in making up hospital garments and rolling bandages, in receiving and distributing sanitary stores, in preparing delicate food for the sick, at its special diet kitchen at Benton Barracks, where 19,382 dishes had been prepared from May 20th to October 1st, 1863, and in assisting the Western Sanitary Commission in its work. Of articles made, up to October 1st, 1863, its report shows 37,676 sheets, 2,664 shirts, 1,765 pairs of drawers, 2,568 bed sacks, 79,324 pillow cases, 3,558 towels, amounting to 127,555 articles. In doing this work soldiers' wives were given employment, and $6,130.85 paid out for the purpose, the articles being used by the Western Sanitary Commission, and the Medical Purveyor. The receipts of the Society, in money alone, up to Sept. 25th, 1863, had been $31,137.42, and its disbursements $28,987.85. Its receipts in sanitary stores have been very great, coming largely from the noble women of St. Louis, and its distributions of the same class of articles issued by the Western Sanitary Commission, to Oct. 1st, 1863, were 225,134 articles.

The Freedmen's Relief Society of St. Louis is a local organization of ladies, who have rendered most useful service and aid in behalf of the poor freedmen, and their families at St. Louis, and in sending contributions to Memphis, Helena, and other points on the lower Mississippi. Their co-operation with the Western Sanitary Commission has been very efficient, and thousands of poor "contrabands," at Benton Barracks, and elsewhere, have had occasion to bless them.

The officers of this association are Mrs. Washington King, *President*, Mrs. Lucien Eaton, *Vice President*, Mrs. C. C. Bailey, *Treasurer*, Mrs. Wm. T. Hazard, *Corresponding Secretary*, and Mrs. Enos Clarke, *Recording Secretary*. Its Board of Managers are Mrs. H. A. Nelson, Mrs.

H. Kennedy, Mrs. O. H. Platte, Mrs. N. Chapman, Mrs. Wm. McKee, Mrs. J. H. Parker, Mrs. Dr. McMurray, Mrs. John McLean, Mrs. Truman Woodruff, Mrs. L. Brawner, Mrs. W. D. Butler, and Miss A. L. Forbes. The following gentlemen are also an advisory committee:—Rev. H. A. Nelson, D.D., Rev. Henry Cox, Lucien Eaton, Esq., and Henry Hitchcock, Esq.

During the summer of 1863, several thousands of freedmen were brought from Helena and elsewhere, to St. Louis, and quartered in the old Missouri Hotel; a hospital was opened for the sick, on Sixth street, and the society had its hands full in assisting to clothe them, and minister to their necessities. Many of these people were afterwards forwarded to Kansas, Iowa, and Illinois, as hired laborers. But a large work still remained for the freedmen's families at Benton Barracks, where there are many rejected recruits, and families of colored soldiers, to be assisted and provided for. A school for colored children is now taught at that place, by Miss Knight, a lady employed by the Western Sanitary Commission, books are furnished, and a similar work of instruction is carried on for the colored soldiers while they remain.

The receipts of this society, for the year 1863, were, in money, $4,863.20, and its expenditures $3,800.36, and its receipts and disbursements in goods, clothing, etc., a large, but unestimated amount. The articles of clothing distributed were 4,356, besides large quantities of linseys, osnaburgs, and blue checks, to be made into garments. Five hundred dollars were also appropriated towards a church and school house, at Island No. 10, and 93 boxes of clothing, were sent to Columbus, Memphis, Helena, Bolivar, Pittsburg Landing, and Benton Barracks.

As the last pages of this work are passing through the press, a noble enterprize is in progress, in this city, for replenishing the funds of the Western Sanitary Commission, and of these kindred and co-operative associations, that they may be enabled to go on with their noble and philanthropic labors, during the continuance of the war. The great fairs that had been held in the large cities of the East, and in Chicago and Cincinnati, in aid of the United States Sanitary Commission, gave nothing to the funds of the Western Commission. Illinois, Indiana, and Ohio, neighboring States, have poured their great and generous contributions chiefly through that channel; and their own regiments, as this history will show, have been the constant care of the Western Sanitary Commission, both in the field and in its Soldier's Homes. With large and increasing demands upon its treasury and supplies, its resources had begun to fail. The example of other cities suggested the idea of a Mississippi Valley Sanitary Fair at St. Louis, and the enterprise was commenced in the latter part of the month of January, by a large preliminary meeting, at Mercantile Library Hall, presided over by the Mayor of the city, Hon. Chauncey I. Filley; at which an organization was effected for this purpose. Speeches were made by the Mayor, by Rev William G. Eliot, D. D., by Brig. Gen'l C. B. Fisk, by Major Gen'l W. S. Rosecrans, by Maj. McKee Dunn, and Professor Amasa McCoy. A letter was read from Lieut. Gen'l Grant, in which he expressed the heartiest sympathy in the undertaking, and bore testimony to the many tons (amounting to thousands,) of sanitary stores furnished to his army by the Western Sanitary Commission. The following officers and committees were then elected, to inaugurate and conduct this great enterprise.

Maj. Gen'l W. S. Rosecrans, *President;* Gov. Willard P. Hall, 1*st Vice President;* Mayor C. I. Filley, 2*d Vice President;* Brig. Gen. C. B. Fisk, 3*d Vice President;* Brig. Gen. J. W. Davidson, 4*th Vice President;* Mayor Jas. S. Thomas, 5*th Vice President;* Sam'l Copp, jr., *Treasurer;* Maj. Alfred Mackay, *Cor. Secretary.*

Standing Committee.—James E. Yeatman, Wm. G. Eliot, George Partridge, Carlos S. Greeley, John B. Johnson,—members of the Western Sanitary Commission.

Executive Committee of Gentlemen.—James E. Yeatman, *Chairman,* J. H. Lightner, E. W. Fox, Sam'l Copp, jr., Geo. D. Hall, S. R.

Filley, Charles B. Hubbell, Jr., James Blackman, Wm. D'Oench, Wm. Patrick, J. O. Pierce, Gustavus W. Dreyer, H. A. Homeyer, B. R. Bonner, Adolphus Meier, Chas. Speck, Wm. Mitchell, Wm. Adriance, George E. Leighton, M. L. Linton, Wm. H. Benton, Dwight Durkee, Amadee Valle, Wyllys King, George P. Plant, Morris Collins, J. C. Cabot, N. C. Chapman, John D. Perry, S. H. Laflin, Jas. Ward.

Executive Committee of Ladies.—Mrs. C. I. Filley, *President;* Miss Anna M. Debenham, *Recording Secretary;* Mr. Gen'l V. P. Van Antwerp, *Corresponding Secretary;* Miss Phœbe W. Couzins, *Corresponding Secretary;* Mrs. Samuel Copp, Jr., *Treasurer;* Mrs. Robert Anderson, Mrs. George Partridge, Mrs. J. E. D. Couzins, Mrs. E. M. Weber, Mrs. Truman Woodruff, Mrs. Clinton B. Fisk, Mrs. F. A. Dick, Mrs. Alfred Clapp, Mrs. Dr. E. Hale, Mrs. A. S. W. Goodwin, Mrs. H. T. Blow, Mrs. Amelia Reihl, Mrs. N. C. Chapman, Mrs. Washington King, Mrs. S. A. Ranlett, Mrs. T. B. Edgar, Mrs. C. S. Greeley, Mrs. W. T. Hazard, Mrs. Charles D. Drake, Mrs. Wm. McKee, Mrs. Samuel C. Davis, Mrs. McKee Dunn, Mrs. R. H. Morton, Mrs. Dr. O'Reilly, Mrs. S. B. Kellogg, Mrs. S. A. Collier, Mrs. W. A. Doan, Mrs. Dr. Hæussler, Mrs. Adolphus Abeles, Mrs. F. P. Blair, Mrs. Elizabeth W. Clarke, Mrs. H. Dreyer, Mrs. John Wolff, Mrs. Ulrich Busch, Mrs. John J. Hoppe, Mrs. Charles Eggers, Mrs. Wm. D'Oench, Mrs. Dr. Hill, Mrs Adolphus Meier, Mrs. John C. Vogel, Mrs. R. Barth, Mrs. H. C. Gempp, Mrs. O. D. Filley, Mrs. Henry Stagg, Mrs. E. W. Fox.

Various subordinate committees were afterwards appointed, representing all the trades and branches of business in St. Louis, and a committee was appointed to conduct a department in the Fair for the benefit of freedmen and Union refugees, so that contributions might be made for this charity, by itself, and kept separate from the general sanitary work of the army.

Appeals were immediately sent out to the people of the Mississippi valley, and to the whole country; the newspaper press of St. Louis lent their columns, with great generosity, to the promotion of the enterprise, and published largely in its interests; and friendly papers abroad have given it all the publicity that could be desired.

The merchants and private citizens, the noble men and women of St. Louis, have taken hold of the enterprise with a generous zeal, and determined to make it a decided success. Friends in Boston, New York, New Bedford, New Haven, have made handsome donations, and some of them have sent representatives to aid in the work. While these labors were being performed, a splendid building was erected on Twelfth Street, from Olive St. to St. Charles St., 500 feet long and 114 feet wide, with wings on Locust street, 100 feet each in length, beyond the main building, and 54 feet wide, with an octagon centre 75 feet in diameter, and 50 feet high. A stereoscopticon has also been built at one side; and the whole has been arranged, decorated, divided into apartments, and filled with contributions from art and nature, of the most valuable kinds. From the mineral and agricultural, and manufacturing resources of Missouri and the great west, from lakes and oceans, and rivers, from battle fields and farms and workshops, and stores of merchandize, gifts have come that make one of the most beautiful and valuable collections that has ever been gathered on this continent.

Besides these contributions in goods, at the opening of the Fair, on the 17th of May, $200,000 in money had already been given towards the object, of which much the largest portion comes from the citizens of St. Louis, a city that has probably suffered more from the war than any of the loyal cities of the Union.

For three days the Fair has been in successful progress, and before it closes, this sketch of the labors and history of the Western Sanitary Commission will be added to its contributions, and explain more fully the great work for which it has been held, and to which its results will be sacredly appropriated. Written under a pressure of other duties, and without opportunity of revision, its chapters going to press as fast as they can be given to the printers, it must needs contain some imperfections and errors, and some omissions will doubtless have occurred; but a frequent demand has been made for such a work, and it is hoped that it will be of some service to the great cause we have at heart, and give to the world a better appreciation of the labors and sacrifices that are necessary to sustain our heroes in the great conflict in which we are engaged—a conflict of the free States of the Republic with the slave-power of the South, which has undertaken to divide our country, build itself up on the ruins of a beneficent Government, and perpetuate, through coming ages, the crime of holding millions of the human race in bondage. In this contest, in which the Providence of a just God is clearly seen, vindicating itself, let it be our part to be found on the side of humanity, of Christian civilization, of liberty and law; and may God save the right!

INDEX.

www.ingramcontent.com/pod-product-compliance
Lightning Source LLC
LaVergne TN
LVHW021408110826
845150LV00007B/1834